MOMENTS *of* DESTINY

ON THE PATHWAY OF LIFE

Five-minute meditations from the Word of God
to encourage God's purpose in your life

by Greg Perkins

©*2000 by Gregory S. Perkins*

Unless otherwise indicated, all scripture references are from the New American Standard Bible (NAS).
©The Lockman Foundation
1960, 1962, 1963, 1968, 1971, 1972, 1973, 1975, 1977.
Library of Congress Control Number: 00-93549
ISBN: 0-9703454-0-2

No part of this book may be reproduced without written permission except for brief quotation in books, newsletters and critical reviews.

Cover Design: Greg Perkins
Cover Photography Copyright © 2000
by Morris Press

Printed in the United States by
Morris Publishing • 3212 East Highway 30 • Kearney, NE 68847
1-800-650-7888

Acknowledgements

...to my wife, DiAnn
There are not words to express the love and appreciation I have for God placing you in my life. Your understanding, patience and your prayers have been a constant encouragement to me. Thank you for supporting me in this effort.

...to my boys, Brad and Alex
You have helped me retain the laughter of my youth. Your quick wit and knack for the humorous have been a blessing in the "moments" of ministry difficulties.

...to my mother
Thank you for believing in me so strongly and for investing your values, your commitment to God, and your never-give-up spirit into my life.

This book is dedicated to my father, Jim Perkins, who taught me more about ministry than I ever realized while he was alive. His unfulfilled desire of being in full-time ministry for the Lord is a mantle that I have carried with me as I have endeavored to fulfill the calling of God in my own life. His unconditional love and support for his family and for the pastors he served is a rare treasure that I continue to cherish.

Table Of Contents

Foreword 5
Love Is A Many "Splintered Thing 9
Six Things Satan Doesn't Want You To Do 12
Customer or Disciple? 15
What Do You Do For A Living? 18
Where Did It Go? 20
Standing In The Wrong Line 23
Breaking Through! 26
Fruit Bearing 101 28
A Mother Should Be... 30
The Herald's Headlines 33
Can You Spare A Digm? 36
Is Life Really Worth Living? 39
Revival! Coming To A Life Near You 42
What Shall I Write This Month? 45
Are You Da' Man? 48
Give Me Liberty Of Give Me Death 51
Back To School Issue 54
Putting The REAL in Religion 56
There's Just Something About That Psalm 58
Faith That Works 61
What To Do When God Is Late 63
Tossing Our Caps Over The Wall 66
Reason To Rejoice 68
The Spirit Of Eleazer.. 70
Do We Need FORM-al Religion? 73
Hope In The Valley 76
My Jesus, My Savior 79
The Sacrifice Of Praise 82
Special Delivery 85
Trying To Do The Job Alone 88
Thirsty Anyone? 91
Help Wanted – Inquire Within 93
Someone's In The Kitchen With Martha 95
Why Sit We Here 'Til They Die? 97
Eyeball To Knee Cap 100
We Need Eleven Heads Of "Let-Us!" 102
Isaiah's Corrected Vision 104
Making Room For God 107
David's Giants 109
Church On The Move? Or Church On The Stay? 112

Foreword

It's Time To...Move On!

Genesis 11:31-12:3
And Terah took Abram his son, and Lot the son of Haran, his grandson, and Sarai his daughter-in-law, his son Abram's wife; and they went out together from Ur of the Chaldeans in order to enter the land of Canaan; and they went as far as Haran, and settled there.

And the days of Terah were two hundred and five years; and Terah died in Haran.

Now the LORD said to Abram, "Go forth from your country, and from your relatives and from your father's house, to the land which I will show you; And I will make you a great nation, and I will bless you, and make your name great; and so you shall be a blessing; And I will bless those who bless you, and the one who curses you I will curse. And in you all the families of the earth shall be blessed." (NAS)

The subject of spiritual destiny is one of great interest to many people today. So much of our world is in a desperate search for purpose and direction. They will often turn to psychics and horoscopes to get some sort of leading for their lives. Friend, you and I must realize that the source of our destiny can only be found in God. He has provided His Word to lead and guide us through life so that we may fulfill the destiny prepared for us.

Paul said in Ephesians 1:17-18, *For I always pray the God of our Lord Jesus Christ, the father of glory, that he may grant you a spirit of wisdom and revelation—of insight into mysteries and secrets—in the [deep and intimate] knowledge of Him, by having the eyes of your heart flooded with light, so that you can know and understand the hope to which he has called you and how rich is His glorious inheritance in the saints—His set apart ones. (Amp)*

Many Christians fail to grasp that God has a purpose—a DESTINY—for their lives. The word destiny has been distorted, misused and overused by the world, and the church has avoided it altogether. Essentially, *destiny* comes from *destine* which is defined: *to set apart (for a specific purpose)*. Another word associated with this concept is *destination*. Destination is *the place to which a person or thing is going*. Friend, God has established a plan—a purpose—a destination for our lives. The DESTINY for our lives is found in the *moments* journeying the path leading to the destination. Every journey is filled with a variety of moments ranging from elation to discouragement. Destiny is achieved by navigating through the moments and reaching the destination.

In Isaiah 55:11 God says, *"so shall my word be that goeth forth out of my mouth: it shall not return unto me void, but it shall accomplish that which I please, and it shall prosper the thing whereunto I sent it.*

Plainly put, each time we receive the Word of God through preaching, teaching or reading, it is being planted into us to accomplish God's will and purpose in our lives— our DESTINY in God!

In His Word, we find the story of Israel and their journey to the "promised land" to help us in our search.

Make no mistake, these mighty people of God were a nation of Destiny. You see, God had a specific plan to be accomplished in their lives—a promise to be fulfilled.

This promise or Destiny was that they would be a people set apart for God to enjoy His blessings and fellowship. Their Destiny was already firmly fixed in the heart of God from the beginning of time, but was revealed to His servant Abram at this appointed time. (Genesis 11:31-12:3) It was time to MOVE ON!

Look at that text for a moment. Notice that Abram's father took the family and "Set out to go to Canaan. But when they got to Haran, they settled there." You see, they were on their way to where God wanted them to go, but settled for another place before they got there. God had to speak to Abram to "MOVE ON!" from the place they had settled for, to go into the place He intended. It was their Destiny and God wanted them to MOVE ON!

This picture describes so many Christians today. God has a destiny for them and they are on their way to fulfill it, but "settle" for something before they get there. In each of our lives, we are on a journey to fulfill our destiny, but are in danger of "settling" before we arrive there.

I believe God is calling the Church to MOVE ON!

To MOVE ON...from our comfort zone. We cannot afford to become comfortable with the status quo, but must press on. Paul said it best in Philippians 3 when he said, "I have not yet attained it...but I forget what is behind and press on toward the goal of the upward calling of God". Abram had to leave the comfort zone he had settled for to fulfill the Destiny God had for Him.

God is calling us to MOVE ON...through our obstacles...

The journey to fulfill our Destiny is not an easy one. Unfortunately, there are a few obstacles to overcome to get where we're going, but God promised to lead us (Gen. 12:1) "to a place I will show you."

Abram faced some difficult challenges in his journey, but with God's help, he made it. There were those who opposed, pushed and doubted him, but he went through!

God is calling us to MOVE ON...into the promise!

If we move from our comfort zones, through the obstacles, but stop before we go into our promise—we fail! Not only will we miss out on the Destiny God has for us, but the generations that follow us will, too.

When Moses led the people out from Egypt and through the wilderness, they stopped before going into the Promised Land. When they did, and entire generation was lost and failed to receive the promise.

We cannot afford to lose an *ENTIRE GENERATION*— not this one—or the one to come.

It's time to...MOVE ON!

Let's move FROM our comfort, THROUGH the obstacles and INTO the Promise God has for us!

This book contains a collection of meditations designed as soul and spirit reminders to help us "run with perseverance, the race marked out for us." If we abandon the journey to our destination, or simply take another path, we cannot ever hope to be in the "place"—the DESTINY—God wants us to enjoy.

In each "moment" of our lives, we take another step on the path of destiny. I pray this book will assist you in watching your step.

Chapter 1

Love Is A Many "Splintered" Thing!

1 Corinthians 13:1-13

If I speak with the tongues of men and of angels, but do not have love, I have become a noisy gong or a clanging cymbal. And if I have the gift of prophecy, and know all mysteries and all knowledge; and if I have all faith, so as to remove mountains, but do not have love, I am nothing. And if I give all my possessions to feed the poor, and if I deliver my body to be burned, but do not have love, it profits me nothing.

Love is patient, love is kind, and is not jealous; love does not brag and is not arrogant, does not act unbecomingly; it does not seek its own, is not provoked, does not take into account a wrong suffered, does not rejoice in unrighteousness, but rejoices with the truth; bears all things, believes all things, hopes all things, endures all things.

Love never fails; but if there are gifts of prophecy, they will be done away; if there are tongues, they will cease; if there is knowledge, it will be done away. For we know in part, and we prophesy in part; but when the perfect comes, the partial will be done away.

When I was a child, I used to speak as a child, think as a child, reason as a child; when I became a man, I did away with childish things. For now we see in a mirror dimly, but then face to face; now I know in part, but then I shall know fully just as I also have been fully known.

But now abide faith, hope, love, these three; but the greatest of these is love. (NAS)

The word and concept of Love is something so misused and misunderstood in our world today. The world's definition is so far from what is real, that many live their lives searching in the wrong places. (*Almost sounds like a country & western song!*)

1 John 3:16 says, "This is how we know what love is. Jesus Christ laid down his life for us." 1 Corinthians 13 paints the picture of what Love looks like and Christ fulfilled it by his death on the cross. No one ever loved us like this. John 15:13 says, *"Greater love hath no man than this, than a man lay down his life for his friends."*

Therefore, Love is symbolized by the Cross—and you cannot handle wood without getting a splinter. In fact, 1 Corinthians 13 will give us FOUR SPLINTERS.

The First Splinter—Represents the **"Profit Margin"**."

What good is it to do all these great, noble and generous things and not have love? It is useless! There's no profit in it!

Businesses are built on philosophies or formulas that determine their profitability in the market place. If they abandon their formula, they will not remain in business.

In the same way, we cannot abandon our formula for success—LOVE. If we do not function in love in our spiritual lives we cannot stay in business. The only way we can function in love (*i.e. have love for others*) is to have received His love. In other words, you can not love until you've been loved—and you haven't been loved until you have been loved by GOD!

The Second Splinter—Represents the **"Passion Paradox"**.

Verses 4-7 tell us what love really is. But it is not at all what the world practices. The world promotes a love that is based upon passion (physical/sexual), but our text doesn't. It isn't even mentioned. *Why?* Because that's not what love is about.

A paradox is something that is not what it seems to be or the opposite of reality. According to the Word of God, the world's version of love is the opposite of God's.

In a manner of speaking—"If <u>this</u> is love then <u>that</u> ain't it!" We would do well to ask ourselves, *"What kind of 'love' do we promote, seek after and live?"*

The Third Splinter--Represents the **"Perpetuation Principle"**.

Verses 8-12 basically say, *<u>love never fails!</u>* Society speaks of "falling into" and "falling out" of love just like a mud puddle or pothole. But God says, "Love <u>never</u> fails!" The word "*never*" makes no provision for variance. Our feelings and emotions change like the wind but God <u>never</u> changes. Simply put, *<u>love doesn't quit!</u>*

God loved us even when we weren't lovely. Romans 5:8 tells us, *"...<u>that, while we were still sinners, Christ died for us</u>."*

The Fourth Splinter--Represents the **"Priority Pursuit"**.

The end of the chapter says, "<u>The greatest of these is love.</u>" It literally means that it should be our main priority in life. We each should pursue a life of love. Love is the foundation that everything else is built upon. Colossians 3 says that over all other virtues, we should put on love because it brings everything together in unity.

In light of these thoughts, don't remove these splinters from your life.

Chapter 2

Six Things Satan Doesn't Want You To Do

Hebrews 10:19-25
Since therefore, brethren, we have confidence to enter the holy place by the blood of Jesus, by a new and living way which He inaugurated for us through the veil, that is, His flesh, and since we have a great priest over the house of God, let us draw near with a sincere heart in full assurance of faith, having our hearts sprinkled clean from an evil conscience and our bodies washed with pure water.

Let us hold fast the confession of our hope without wavering, for He who promised is faithful; and let us consider how to stimulate one another to love and good deeds, not forsaking our own assembling together, as is the habit of some, but encouraging one another; and all the more, as you see the day drawing near.
(NAS)

When mankind fell in the Garden of Eden, a lot of things changed. BUT...some things stayed the same. First, God is still God—He's the same yesterday, today and forever. And second, Satan is still a liar!

He tempted Adam and Eve by deceiving them. *"Did God really say, 'You must not eat from any tree in the garden'?" "You will not surely die," the serpent said to the woman. "For God knows that when you eat of it your eyes will be opened, and you will be like God, knowing good and evil."* (Gen. 3:1, 4 & 5 *NIV*)

Satan has been the same ever since. He says it's left, when it's really right. He says down, when it's really up. The Scripture says that he doesn't hold to the truth, because there is no truth in him—and that he is not only a liar, but the father of lies!

Mark it down, if Satan wants you to do something—you'd better not do it. The opposite is also true. If Satan doesn't want you to do something—you'd better do it, because he's a liar and cannot tell the truth.

Satan does not want you to succeed. It says in John 10:10 that he came to steal, and to kill, and to destroy, but Jesus came to give life, and that more abundantly!

Let's look at some things that the devil doesn't want you to do and you can rest assured that if the devil doesn't want you to do them—GOD DOES!

1. *Satan doesn't want you to go to church.* Why? Because God wants you there. Heb. 10:25 says to not forsake the gathering of ourselves together. Satan doesn't want you to be in church because he knows that you will be encouraged. He knows that the Word of God will be preached, and that the Holy Spirit will have opportunity to convince and convict you of sin and to reveal to you the things of God.

2. *Satan doesn't want you to pray.* Why? Because God wants you to pray. Satan knows that prayer brings power, it brings victory, and that it brings "peace that surpasses our own understanding." (Phil. 4:7)

3. *Satan doesn't want you to witness.* Why? Because God does. Satan knows that when people hear the gospel, they will be drawn by the Holy Spirit. He also knows that when you share your faith, your faith becomes stronger.

4. *Satan doesn't want you to trust God.* Why? Because he knows that when people trust God they lose all fear. He also knows that when they trust God, they will stop believing satan's lies!

5. *Satan doesn't want you to read the Bible.* Why? Because the Word reveals God's will, and Satan likes to keep you confused. He knows that God's Word tells us about him and his deceit, and that God's Word tells the truth!

6. *Satan doesn't want you to yield to the Holy Spirit.* Why? Because Satan knows that there is real joy in being led by the Spirit, and that the Holy Spirit empowers us with authority over sin and the powers of darkness.

Satan's greatest nightmare is a group of church going, praying, witnessing, trusting, Bible reading, Spirit-led people. They are people who cannot be defeated by his schemes and deceit.

Now that you have heard what Satan doesn't want you to do—what do you think God does want you to do?

Chapter 3

Customer Or Disciple?

Luke 9:12-17
And the day began to decline, and the twelve came and said to Him, "Send the multitude away, that they may go into the surrounding villages and countryside and find lodging and get something to eat; for here we are in a desolate place."

But He said to them, "You give them something to eat!" And they said, "We have no more than five loaves and two fish, unless perhaps we go and buy food for all these people." (For there were about five thousand men.) And He said to His disciples, "Have them recline to eat in groups of about fifty each."

And they did so, and had them all recline. And He took the five loaves and the two fish, and looking up to heaven, He blessed them, and broke them, and kept giving them to the disciples to set before the multitude.

And they all ate and were satisfied; and the broken pieces which they had left over were picked up, twelve baskets full.
(NAS)

There is a bit of information that has always troubled me about Luke chapter 9. The Scripture tells us in verse 14, that there were 5,000 people present at the "feeding." Jesus takes 5 loaves and 2 small fish and feeds 5,000 men as well as the estimated 10,000 women and children that were present.

You might ask, "Why are you troubled over that?" Well, when I turn to Acts chapters 1 and 2, I see that there were only 120 present seeking the Holy Spirit.

Church growth experts would say, "Hey Jesus, you've got a problem. You let 4,550 people slip through the cracks!"

Something was indeed wrong. One week they were shouting "Hosanna!" and the next week, "Crucify Him!"

How can this be? I read an article written by Joel Pavia, a church leader in Wisconsin, and it contained an illustration I'd like to share with you.

When the Communist Party took over Romania many years ago, some of the evangelical pastors decided to embrace Communism. In fact, a few of them became leaders in the party. One of the pastors that stayed true, Pastor Wurmbrandt, was extremely troubled by the action of his fellow pastors and asked God how they could embrace Communism. God spoke to him and told him, *"some people go to the bakery to buy bread, others go to learn the craft."*

It appears that some of these individuals were customers while others were willing to become disciples. When Communism came along with its offers, claims and promises, they switched from Christianity to Communism because they were just "getters"—customers—not disciples.

If I only remain a customer at the bakery I can complain about the bread. *Not enough salt, too much salt, crust is too hard or too soft.* I could quit going to that bakery and go to another and another. But if I'm in the back baking the bread, then I am committed and will do all that I can to make the best bread I can.

If we only go to church to get something, we are customers. If we go to give of ourselves we then become disciples. Customers remain faithful as long as they can get what they want. They often come with the premise, "If I can get blessed, count me in—but if this is going to cost me something, count me out!"

If a Christian only interprets the cross as to how it benefits him and works for his safety, security and victory, he misses much of the teaching of discipleship. God wants us to embrace the way of the cross. It is where self has been crossed out and as Christians we live to give, share, die, give up, and surrender. Self always wants to be something or someone. It is, *"The customer is always right"* syndrome.

At times, Jesus' disciples wanted to know which of them would be the greatest. Jesus said they should be the least and become servants.

We all come into this family as customer, but let's not stay long in that stage. We must go on to become disciples.

Some go to buy bread; some go to bake bread. Those baking are too busy to get caught up in complaining.

Customer or Disciple? *Interesting question. Which would you say that you are?*

Chapter 4

What Do You Do For A Living?

Psalm 150:1-6
Praise the LORD! Praise God in His sanctuary; praise Him in His mighty expanse. Praise Him for His mighty deeds; praise Him according to His excellent greatness. Praise Him with trumpet sound; praise Him with harp and lyre. Praise Him with timbrel and dancing; praise Him with stringed instruments and pipe. Praise Him with loud cymbals; praise Him with resounding cymbals.

Let everything that has breath praise the LORD. Praise the LORD! (NAS)

No doubt you have been asked the common question, "What do you do for a living?" Most people gladly answer that question with a certain amount of pride in what they do. One man was asked the question, to which he replied, "I breathe!"

It Sounds like a "smart alec" response, but if you think about the basic truth of the statement, it is a reality. In order for our bodies to perform the most basic functions, we must breathe.

Breathing is an amazing process. It is so basic to our nature that we do it without thinking, and yet, if we were to stop breathing, it is all we can think about – just getting the next breath. In its simplest form, life and death are separated by just one breath.

Breathing is natural because it is essential, just as our praise to God is essential! Psalm 150:6 says, "Let everything that has breath praise the Lord!" In light of the things we have just stated, that includes everyone that is alive. I breathe, therefore, I <u>must</u> praise God! No one is exempt from honoring God with their praise.

In 1 Thessalonians 4:18, the Apostle Paul tells us to, *"give thanks in all circumstances..."* because it is God's will for our lives! Then the writer of Hebrews tells us in chapter 13:15 to *"...continually offer to God a sacrifice of praise...the fruit of lips that confess His name"* as Lord of our lives. This means that praise is the fruit (produce/product) of our mouths.

The Word is clear. If we are alive (breathing) and we confess His name (i.e. Christians), then it is the will of God in our lives that we praise Him as a natural function of our existence.

Lest you think that the only one benefited by praise is God, listen to the bit of news in 2 Chronicles 20:15-22. We find the people of God facing a vast enemy seeking to destroy their very existence—take the breath from them. God spoke to them in verse 17 and told them to take their positions (be where they were supposed to be), stand still, and see the salvation or rescue of the Lord on their behalf. In verses 21 and 22, it says that they appointed men to sing praises to the Lord at the head of the army. As they went forth, the Lord set ambushes for their enemies and defeated them. Praise not only pleases God, but also brings victory to the life of the one that praises!

Each time you come to the house of God, come prepared to praise Him. The more you praise Him, the more natural it will become until it's just like taking a breath. You will praise Him continually without being aware of it.

Chapter 5
Where Did It Go?

Judges 16:4-21

After this it came about that he loved a woman in the valley of Sorek, whose name was Delilah. And the lords of the Philistines came up to her, and said to her, "Entice him, and see where his great strength lies and how we may overpower him that we may bind him to afflict him. Then we will each give you eleven hundred pieces of silver."

So Delilah said to Samson, "Please tell me where your great strength is and how you may be bound to afflict you."

15...Then she said to him, "How can you say, 'I love you,' when your heart is not with me? You have deceived me these three times and have not told me where your great strength is." And it came about when she pressed him daily with her words and urged him, that his soul was annoyed to death.

So he told her all that was in his heart...

18...When Delilah saw that he had told her all that was in his heart, she sent and called the lords of the Philistines, saying, "Come up once more, for he has told me all that is in his heart." Then the lords of the Philistines came up to her, and brought the money in their hands. And she made him sleep on her knees, and called for a man and had him shave off the seven locks of his hair. Then she began to afflict him, and his strength left him.

And she said, "The Philistines are upon you, Samson!" And he awoke from his sleep and said, "I will go out as at other times and shake myself free." But he did not know that the LORD had departed from him.

Then the Philistines seized him and gouged out his eyes; and they brought him down to Gaza and bound him with bronze chains, and he was a grinder in the prison. (NAS)

Why is it that summer passes by so swiftly? It seems the kids just get out of school, when suddenly we find ourselves back in the "swing" of things with vacations ended and kids back in the classroom.

The flurry of activity makes us so busy that before we know it, the leaves have turned, fallen, and are scattered across our brown lawns. We then ask ourselves, "Where did it go, and what did I do with it?"

It reminds me of a Bible truth shared in Judges 16. It tells of a young man with great strength and tremendous potential for God. He started well, but success fed his ego until he strayed from the promises of God. Being an impulsive individual, he often did what first came to his mind. Of course, that was not always the best or even godly thing to do.

You've already figured that I am speaking of Samson. You see, his strength was the result of God's presence in his life—and God's presence was a result of honoring his vows to Him.

As we pick up the account in Judges 16, the only unbroken vow in Samson's life was relating to the cutting of his hair. Therein was the secret of his strength. It was at this point in his life that he met the lovely Delilah who was hired by the Philistines to lure the secret of his strength from him.

On three occasions she set a trap, and each time found that Samson had tricked her. On the fourth try, she finally wore him down through her nagging (v.17).

You see, each time he tricked her, he got closer to the truth, until he finally gave in. It was the pattern of his life. The vows of his existence were traded one by one for moments of pleasure and happiness. Each time, he toyed with the gift of God's strength and presence, until it was all gone. Verse 20 says, "He awoke from his sleep and thought, 'I'll go on as before and shake myself free.' But he did not know the Lord had left him."

This is a tragedy not only because of Samson's defeat, but because this story is repeated day after day in our world. It seems we become so pre-occupied with the life that we are living—with its hectic schedules, possessions, relationships, and "reward"—that we lose sight of our real purpose in life which is **TO HONOR GOD**! We place God, His house, and His Word in the back seat while we pursue our own impulses and desires. With each compromise, we draw nearer to waking from sleep as we always have before, only to discover that His presence is gone—not even aware that he had left us!

Before we find ourselves looking out upon our brown lawns scattered with fallen leaves, and asking, *"Where did it go?"* we must adjust our priorities. What is more important in your life? The presence of more things—more people—and more activities? Or the *Presence of Almighty God?*

Chapter 6

Standing In The Wrong Line!

Hebrews 4:1-11

Therefore, let us fear lest, while a promise remains of entering His rest, any one of you should seem to have come short of it.

For indeed we have had good news preached to us, just as they also; but the word they heard did not profit them, because it was not united by faith in those who heard.

For we who have believed enter that rest, just as He has said, "As I swore in My wrath, they shall not enter My rest," although His works were finished from the foundation of the world.

For He has thus said somewhere concerning the seventh day, "And God rested on the seventh day from all His works", and again in this passage, "They shall not enter My rest."

Since therefore it remains for some to enter it, and those who formerly had good news preached to them failed to enter because of disobedience,

He again fixes a certain day, "Today," saying through David after so long a time just as has been said before, "Today if you hear His voice, do not harden your hearts."

For if Joshua had given them rest, He would not have spoken of another day after that. There remains therefore a Sabbath rest for the people of God.

For the one who has entered His rest has himself also rested from his works, as God did from His.

Let us therefore be diligent to enter that rest, lest anyone fall through following the same example of disobedience. (NAS)

There is probably no more frustrating experience than to stand in the long line at the Tag Office only to discover that you didn't have all the necessary documents to have your license plates renewed. Or to find out after standing in line for many hours that you were in the wrong line.

Hebrews 4:1 warns us that we are to be careful (give attention) lest we "fall short." In other words, we must be careful how we live so that at the end of life we don't find ourselves "in the wrong line."

Many Christians today are standing in the wrong line. They have become comfortable with luke-warm Christianity. And because of their spiritual neglect, they do not even realize that they aren't in the right place.

Allow me to use the art of reverse psychology in the sharing of some important thoughts with "Seven Ways To Be Sure You're In The *Wrong* Line!"

1. ***Listen to the preacher***, but don't respond. You wouldn't want him to get a "big head", and if you ignore him, he'll probably stop preaching like that.

2. ***NEVER volunteer for anything!*** Someone will eventually do it--they always do.

3. ***Try not to attend EVERY service***, People will think that you're a fanatic, and that you actually like that religious stuff.

4. ***Complain A Lot!*** Make sure everyone knows how unhappy you are as often as possible. After all, if you're thinking it, you might as well say it!

5. ***Hold on to EVERY dollar you can.*** You've worked hard for your money, and those people can help themselves.

6. ***Avoid being alone with God as much as possible.*** That way he can't ask you to do anything silly.

7. ***NEVER do anything that might make you look funny.*** You have a reputation to think about.

Of course, you realize that the reverse should really be our course of action as Christian men and women. None of us would set about adhering to a list of actions as previously listed. And yet, by not doing what God has called us to do in His Word—we actually fulfill them by default.

Through neglect, we "fall short" of what God intends for us as His children. And through neglect, we become oblivious to the fact that we are actually standing in the wrong line.

If we do not give attention to these matters in our spiritual life, we may find ourselves standing (in line) before God and hear Him say, *"Depart from me..."* (Mt. 25:41) The passage in Matthew 25 is a riveting account of separation between sheep and goats. Jesus replied in verse 45 by saying, *"I tell you the truth, whatever you did not do for one of the least of these, you did not do for me."*

It's not so much what they've DONE—but what they HAVEN'T done. James 4:17 says *"Anyone then, who knows the good he ought to do and doesn't do it, sins!"*

What line are you standing in today? Is everything in order in your life, so that when you stand before Him, He responds, *"Well done! Thou good and faithful servant."* Instead of—*"I'm sorry, you're in the wrong line!"*

Chapter 7

Breaking Through!

Philippians 3:13-21
> Brethren, I do not regard myself as having laid hold of it yet; but one thing I do: forgetting what lies behind and reaching forward to what lies ahead, I press on toward the goal for the prize of the upward call of God in Christ Jesus.
> Let us therefore, as many as are perfect, have this attitude; and if in anything you have a different attitude, God will reveal that also to you; however, let us keep living by that same standard to which we have attained.
> Brethren, join in following my example, and observe those who walk according to the pattern you have in us.
> For many walk, of whom I often told you, and now tell you even weeping, that they are enemies of the cross of Christ, whose end is destruction, whose god is their appetite, and whose glory is in their shame, who set their minds on earthly things.
> For our citizenship is in heaven, from which also we eagerly wait for a Savior, the Lord Jesus Christ; who will transform the body of our humble state into conformity with the body of His glory, by the exertion of the power that He has even to subject all things to Himself. (NAS)

If you are anything like me, you didn't accomplish everything on your "to do" list last year, and the odds of completing it this year are pretty slim. Well, how will you "BREAK THROUGH" this year?

Philippians 3:13-14 tells us to forget what is behind and press on!

We cannot go back and rewrite the events of the past year. So what can we do? **PRESS ON!**

There will be a host of opportunities and challenges before us. There will be a temptation to give up and get sidetracked from our goals to break through in the coming year, but we must heed the words of the Apostle Paul to **PRESS ON!**

1. PRESS ON Through Discouragement. Things will not always go your way. There will be days that you will wish you could go back to bed and start over, but you must PRESS ON!

Job could have given up after losing everything he had in a single day. He could have listened to his wife who said, "Curse God and die!" But he chose to trust God and said, "Though He slay me, yet will I trust in Him." (Job 13:15)

2. PRESS ON Through Discipline. Hebrews 12:11 says *"No discipline seems pleasant at the time!"* (Understatement?) It goes on to say that it produces Righteousness and Peace!

The lack of discipline in a person's life will lead to a host of problems. We have to learn to do the hard things in life instead of taking the easy way. We must learn to say NO to self and the natural desires that try to lead us away from the things of God

3. PRESS ON Through Delight. Watch out when everything is going well. We find ourselves not being as careful as we should.

2 Corinthians 10:12 says *"Take heed when you think you are standing, LEST YOU FALL."* You see, we stop trusting in God when everything is going our way. Look at the church of Laodocia found in Revelation 3. They thought they had it all and became lukewarm in their spiritual lives. They stopped trusting in God and started trusting in themselves. That is a recipe for disaster.

Paul said "I do not regard myself as having laid hold of it (the prize) yet, but one thing I do: forgetting what is behind and reaching forward to what lies ahead." What he was simply saying was—"I'm not there yet, so I must keep on going!" We must develop the same determination if we will "break through" to the things God has for us.

Chapter 8
Fruit Bearing 101

John 15:1-8 & 16
"I am the true vine, and My Father is the vinedresser.

"Every branch in Me that does not bear fruit, He takes away; and every branch that bears fruit, He prunes it, that it may bear more fruit.

"You are already clean because of the word which I have spoken to you.

"Abide in Me, and I in you. As the branch cannot bear fruit of itself, unless it abides in the vine, so neither can you, unless you abide in Me.

"I am the vine, you are the branches; he who abides in Me, and I in him, he bears much fruit; for apart from Me you can do nothing.

"If anyone does not abide in Me, he is thrown away as a branch, and dries up; and they gather them, and cast them into the fire, and they are burned.

"If you abide in Me, and My words abide in you, ask whatever you wish, and it shall be done for you.

"By this is My Father glorified, that you bear much fruit, and so prove to be My disciples.

"You did not choose Me, but I chose you, and appointed you, that you should go and bear fruit, and that your fruit should remain, that whatever you ask of the Father in My name, He may give to you. (NAS)

The Bible records Christ as saying, "You did not choose me, but I have chosen you to bear fruit...fruit that will last!" (John 15:16)

I believe there are two things to consider on the subject of spiritual fruitfulness—The Command and the Conditions.

The Command To Fruitfulness...

According to John 15:16, the reason we were chosen was to be fruitful. Fruit is essentially the sign of life within. We must show the life that Christ has given us by bearing fruit. Colossians 1:10 says, that we must please the Lord—bearing fruit in every good work as well as growing in the knowledge of the Lord.

The Conditions To Fruitfulness...

The *First condition* to a fruitful life is **Contact with the Living Water.** Psalm 1 talks about being a tree planted by rivers of living water. No plant or tree will survive without contact with a water source. Our source according to John 6:35 is The Living Water...Jesus Christ!

The *Second condition* to a fruitful life is **Spiritual Receptivity.** The soil must be ready to receive the water and nutrition. Matthew 13:25 tells us that the seed sown in good soil is the man that hears the Word of God and understands it. We must have a teachable spirit and receive the instruction of the Lord

The *Third condition* is **Pruning**. Branches that do not bear fruit are pruned (trimmed) so that they can be fruitful. We must allow the dead unproductive parts of our lives to be cut off that we may be fruitful.

The *Fourth condition* is to **Abide in Christ**. John 15:5 tells us that we cannot be fruitful unless we remain attached to the vine (God) that is our source! In fact, if we detach ourselves, the Word tells us that we can do **nothing!**

More than ever, the church needs fruitful Christians who will bear fruit that glorifies God. Our world is starving to experience productive Christianity that can give it hope in the midst of its situation.

Here's something to consider. If your Christian life produced actual fruit (apples, bananas, etc.), would there be enough fruit to feed anyone?

Chapter 9

A Mother Should Be...

Proverbs 31:28-31
Her children rise up and bless her; her husband also, and he praises her, saying:
"Many daughters have done nobly, but you excel them all."
Charm is deceitful and beauty is vain, but a woman who fears the LORD, she shall be praised.
Give her the product of her hands, and let her works praise her in the gates. (NAS)

I am only a father and husband, but in this moment together I'd like to instruct you in "what a mother should be."

Proverbs 31 is the only extensive teaching to mothers. I believe there are many other texts that compliment this passage and show us what a mother should be.

A Mother Should Be...MINDFUL!

A mother should be mindful or aware that her task is honorable and that the influence she has upon her husband and children is powerful. 2 Chron 22:3 tells us of Ahab and Jezebel's son. "He too walked in the ways of the house of Ahab, for his mother encouraged/influenced him in doing wrong." The mother typically sets the tone within the home.

A Mother Should Be...HELPFUL!

Just as Jezebel contributed to the wickedness of her son and just as Herod's wife prompted her daughter to ask for the head of John the Baptist on a platter—it is in a mother's control to be helpful or hurtful.

Mothers need to concentrate their efforts on helping their children to grow and mature—not to contribute to their destruction by being permissive or uninvolved. Leaving them to raise themselves brings disgrace upon the mother and the child. (Pr 29:15)

A Mother Should Be... WATCHFUL!
A mother should be alert to the dangers that surround her home and family. Peter warns that we should all be self-controlled and alert because our enemy (the devil) is looking for an opportunity to devour us. (1 Peter 5:8)

A mother must also be watchful of the words, attitudes and actions that she displays before her family.

A Mother Should Be... JOYFUL!
When you look at all you do for your family as a drudgery—as work with no purpose—and find no joy in it; no one else will find joy in it either!

The Scripture tells us that wherever the presence of the Lord is, there is joy! When Christ faced the cross, He endured it because of "...the joy set before him..."

A mother that spends time in the presence of God will have joy. Psalm 16:11 "You have made known to me the paths of life. You fill me with joy in your presence."

A Mother Should Be... HOPEFUL!
Filled with hope because of Christ's coming. Filled with hope because of all that he holds in store for her family. A mother with no hope finds it difficult to be at peace—and a mother that is not at peace causes a home to be without peace.

Without hope, everything is meaningless. Hebrews 6:19 tells us that our hope—when founded upon Christ—is the anchor of our soul.

A Mother Should Be...THANKFUL!
Psalm 127:3 tells us that sons are a heritage from the Lord—a reward from Him. To be a mother is to be blessed of the Lord. Thessalonians 5:18 tells us that we are to give thanks in all circumstances—for this is the will of God.

Motherhood is hard indeed, but from what I'm told, it is worthwhile. Mother's Day may occur in May, but our appreciation of our mothers should last ALL YEAR long! They're worth it.

Chapter 10

The "Herald's" Headlines

Luke 2:8-14
> *And in the same region there were some shepherds staying out in the fields, and keeping watch over their flock by night.*
> *And an angel of the Lord suddenly stood before them, and the glory of the Lord shone around them; and they were terribly frightened.*
> *And the angel said to them, "Do not be afraid; for behold, I bring you good news of a great joy which shall be for all the people; for today in the city of David there has been born for you a Savior, who is Christ the Lord.*
> *"And this will be a sign for you: you will find a baby wrapped in cloths, and lying in a manger."*
> *And suddenly there appeared with the angel a multitude of the heavenly host praising God, and saying, "Glory to God in the highest, and on earth peace among men with whom He is pleased." (NAS)*

This passage of Scripture has been preached from pulpits, recited in Christmas productions, and read aloud in family gatherings for centuries. But have we given much thought of its meaning? I believe we often brush past these verses without feeling the true power contained in them.

Imagine what headlines the angel's words would have made in the Bethlehem Herald the next morning if they had been reported. *Good news* of *Great Joy* for *All People!*

Why was it Good News?

I believe it was good news because... **Their past** was filled with disobedience that led to their destruction as a nation. **Their present** condition was that they were people who no longer could rule themselves. They were under the domination of others. **Their Future** was lacking hope.

They were a defeated people. They had looked for the Messiah for many years and had no doubt begun to despair that he would ever come.

This was good news because their past was filled with bad news. This was good news because their present was filled with bad news. This was good news because their future was filled with bad news. *IT WAS GOOD NEWS!*

Why was it Great Joy?

It was great joy because the Messiah had come! Isaiah 61 said that He was the Anointed One who would come and preach the gospel, bind up the broken hearted and set at liberty those who were captive.

It was great joy because redemption had come! Romans 3:24 tells us that we are justified freely by his grace through the redemption that comes through Christ Jesus. 1 Corinthians 1:30 tells us that He became redemption—the purchase price!

It was great joy because New Life had come into the world! What they had and what we have is not life. Without Christ, we have no life—no hope—and no future! But because of this baby born in a manger—we have New Life!

There was reason for great joy because the promise of the Messiah was being fulfilled. Their lives would be redeemed from eternal destruction. *It was Great Joy!*

Why All People?

This was not an exclusive thing. All of mankind would see salvation. Acts 2:21 says *"Everyone who calls upon the name of the Lord shall be saved."* According to 1 Timothy 2:24, *"He wanted ALL men to be saved and come to the knowledge of the truth."* Then Peter told us that *"He is not willing that any should perish, but that ALL should come to repentance."* It was for ALL People!

For those who get frustrated at Christmas, and maybe wonder what all the fuss is about, I encourage you to go to Luke 2:8-14 and find your focus again.

People in this world need some **GOOD NEWS** to reverse all the BAD news they have in their lives. Their past, their present and their future is a constant reminder of what is wrong. All they've had is BAD news—it is time they received the GOOD NEWS that Christ has come to set them free.

People in this world need **GREAT JOY** in their lives. Just spend some time in a shopping mall in the weeks leading up to Christmas and you'll find a lot of people who need joy. Because Christ came, people can be free of the pain, brokenness, and bitterness of their lives!

It is for ***ALL People***! No one is excluded from experiencing God's love.

Maybe if the Bethlehem Herald did report the news, those around would have still missed it, but let us be sure that we do not miss it!

Chapter 11

Can You Spare A Digm?

Mark 16:15-18
> And He said to them, "Go into all the world and preach the gospel to all creation.
> "He who has believed and has been baptized shall be saved; but he who has disbelieved shall be condemned.
> "And these signs will accompany those who have believed: in My name they will cast out demons, they will speak with new tongues; they will pick up serpents, and if they drink any deadly poison, it shall not hurt them; they will lay hands on the sick, and they will recover." (NAS)

No, I didn't misspell "dime." I'm referring to the word "paradigm." What is that? Well, we'll get to it in a moment.

At some point, someone has approached us down on his or her luck looking for change, and they ask "Hey Buddy!" Can you spare a dime?" When faced with that question we either respond or run.

Well, in the church today, we are faced with a world down on its luck—looking for change. They don't necessarily need the change from our pockets, but a change in their lives. People who are lonely, hurting, empty, and disillusioned by the world are looking for change!

As the church, we must help. WE have the answer for lonely and hurting people. He's Jesus! He's the friend that sticks closer than a brother, the one who fills the emptiness and the mender of broken hearts.

You see, the church must be a "change agent" in the lives of those who need it. They cannot change themselves—they need help. God has called us to bring change to our world.

To this point, most of you could agree with what I've shared and even shout an "AMEN," but wait...there's more.

Determining we have the answer, however, is the easy part. How do we get it to those who need it? I contend, if the church is to become effective in being "change agents" for the world, we are going to have to change first!

For too long, we have formulated our programs and meetings and then waited for the world to come find us. We have essentially *expected* the world to come find us, and then *expected* them to change themselves to fit what we are offering.

If Christ had utilized this way of doing ministry, the Samaritan woman would not have found the change she needed. You see, Christ met her where she was. He went out of his way to meet with her.

The Samaritan woman would have never darkened the doors of a "church," because she was not looking for programs and meetings. She was looking for something that could bring real change in her life. That "something" will not be found in a church that is focused upon ministry to itself—but one focused upon ministry to others!

If your church is to become the type of church that can reach the Samaritan-woman-type person, then it will demand that we change our way of thinking about ministry.

Remember our word "paradigm?" It is basically a set of rules and regulations that helps to define boundaries for a group or individual, and determines what must be done to be successful within those boundaries.

Doug Murren, in his book *LeaderShift*, refers to a paradigm as the "tissue paper pattern used by a seamstress." The pattern is made up of a number of pieces that when pieced together correctly, makes a whole garment. The fabric of the garment will be cut using the pattern.

You see, the way we think of church and what the purpose of church is, affects the products that result.

Friend, if we focus upon caring only for us and our needs—tailoring our ministries to meet our own needs—then those who really need ministry cannot receive it until they become one of us and "fit our patterns." On the other hand, if the church focuses upon the needs of those who truly need change in their lives, then *they* are the pattern that we fashion the garment from. With that "mind set" or paradigm for ministry, we will reach them where they are.

The mission of the church compels us to *evangelize, disciple, worship* and *fellowship*. Our purpose drives us to share His love with those around us. Our desire must be to reach our community with ministry that is practical and fitting to their needs!

Can we "Spare a Digm?" Or more plainly, can we "Spare Some Change?'" Are we willing to change our mind set (our paradigm) in order to reach our generation with the message of Christ?

Christ said "Go ye into all the world" and not, "wait for all the world to come to you." If Christ had not come to Samaria—the woman at the well would only have gotten a bucket of water. But, because Christ went to her, her life was "changed" forever!

Chapter 12

Is Life Really Worth Living?

Ps 38:1-15
O LORD, rebuke me not in Thy wrath; and chasten me not in Thy burning anger. For Thine arrows have sunk deep into me, and Thy hand has pressed down on me.

There is no soundness in my flesh because of Thine indignation; there is no health in my bones because of my sin. For my iniquities are gone over my head; as a heavy burden they weigh too much for me. My wounds grow foul and fester. Because of my folly,

I am bent over and greatly bowed down; I go mourning all day long. For my loins are filled with burning; and there is no soundness in my flesh. I am benumbed and badly crushed; I groan because of the agitation of my heart.

Lord, all my desire is before Thee; and my sighing is not hidden from Thee. My heart throbs, my strength fails me; and the light of my eyes, even that has gone from me. My loved ones and my friends stand aloof from my plague; and my kinsmen stand afar off.

Those who seek my life lay snares for me; and those who seek to injure me have threatened destruction, and they devise treachery all day long.

But I, like a deaf man, do not hear; and I am like a dumb man who does not open his mouth.

Yes, I am like a man who does not hear, and in whose mouth are no arguments. For I hope in Thee, O LORD; Thou wilt answer, O Lord my God. (NAS)

In every life, there are times of discouragement. Times when things don't go like we've planned, or when they just plain blow up in our faces. It is in those times that we might ask ourselves, "Is life worth all this?"

If you've done this, you're not alone. You have the company of some of the most well known personalities in Scripture.

Jonah sat under a vine and declared that it would be better if he would die.

Elijah sat under a Juniper and shouted, *"Lord, take me!"*

And David—the great king—pours out his soul in Psalm 38. In verses 1 through 14, he lists all the things that overwhelm him. *"Your hand has come down on me...there is no health in my body...my guilt has overwhelmed me...my wounds fester...and all day I go about mourning."* In verse 7 and 8 he lists one we could all identify with. *"MY back is filled with searing pain... I groan in anguished heart."* In verse 11 he says, *"Is life really worth all this?"* And we might be inclined to agree with him.

David would be right—Life is NOT worth living, if that's all there is!

Each year, thousands of people decide life is not worth living, and seek to end their lives. They are right too...IF life is lived for...

FORTUNE: Jay Gould, the multi-millionaire, said, "I am the most miserable man on this earth." Ivan Kruger, wealthy head of the world's largest monopoly committed suicide.

FAME: "I walk through life thinking I am happy and knowing I am not." Said the famous essayist Charles Lamb. Stephen Foster, composer "Old Black Joe," "Swanee River," and other plantation songs died a drunkard's death at age 38. Poet Edgar Allan Poe drank himself to death.

POWER: Napoleon died a lonely death on the isle where he was exiled, and Julius Caesar was assassinated. Mussolini was executed.

PLEASURE: Recent well-known celebrities John Belushi, Chris Farley and Phil Hartman have found that there is a great deal of pain that goes along with the "pleasures" of this world.

But Life IS worth living if you live it for Christ! The Apostle Paul said, "To LIVE IS Christ, and to die is gain." (Phil 2:21)

Even David changed his tune when he focused upon God instead of the *"things"* of life. Psalm 40 says, *"... he (God) turned to me and heard my cry. He lifted me out of the slimy pit, out of the mud and mire; he set my feet on a rock and gave me a firm place to stand. He put a new song in my mouth, a hymn of praise to our God."*

You see, when you're focused upon the right things, **Life IS worth living!**

Chapter 13

Revival! Coming To A Life Near You--Will it be Yours?

Psalms 85

Lord, You have been favorable to Your land; You have brought back the captivity of Jacob. You have forgiven the iniquity of Your people; You have covered all their sin. Selah

You have taken away all Your wrath; You have turned from the fierceness of Your anger.

Restore us, O God of our salvation, and cause Your anger toward us to cease. Will You be angry with us forever? Will You prolong Your anger to all generations? Will You not revive us again, that Your people may rejoice in You?

Show us Your mercy, O Lord, and grant us Your salvation.

I will hear what God the Lord will speak, For He will speak peace To His people and to His saints; but let them not turn back to folly. Surely His salvation is near to those who fear Him, That glory may dwell in our land.

Mercy and truth have met together; Righteousness and peace have kissed each other. Truth shall spring out of the earth, And righteousness shall look down from heaven.

Yes, the Lord will give what is good; And our land will yield its increase. Righteousness will go before Him, and shall make His footsteps our pathway. (NKJV)

It's easy to talk about revival. We talk about how we want revival in our lives, we talk about how badly our church needs revival, or how someone else needs revival in his/her life.

What about you? Is it easy for you to talk about revival, but it seems to pass you by? Do you legitimately crave the move of God in your life, but it seems to evade you?

It's a common problem, due to a common misconception about revival. As long as we see revival as an **EVENT** or as something that just moves **UPON** us—it will evade us.

Revival is **NOT** an **EVENT**. You can plan dates on a calendar, advertise the moving of God and invite an anointed evangelist, but if the people who attend do not come prepared to **RECEIVE** revival in their heart, everyone will leave disappointed.

The people of God must be prepared in order for anything productive or lasting to occur.

What will it take? How will we experience this revival in our lives? In order to be prepared for revival you must have...

1. <u>**A desire for change.**</u> If you don't have a desire for things to change in YOUR life—revival will evade you. We want change to come to OTHER people, but NOT us. My Pastor, my church, my spouse, the person down the pew—but NOT us.

2. <u>**A heart seeking God's presence.**</u> When you want to see the face of God, and live in his presence—revival will occur in your life. Many people never seek His presence because all the things going on in their lives distract them. When the call is given to come to an altar they don't come forward because they have OTHER things to do.

3. <u>**A mouth filled with praise**</u>—not filled with gossip, negative talk or unwholesome language—but filled with praise. We must praise and lift up His name. Our praises not only glorify Him, but bring defeat to the enemy of our souls (2 Chron 20). All too often we come to a church service and expect to be entertained. We expect others to keep us interested. When we praise Him, He inhabits—or dwells—with us. Things get interesting in our lives when the Master shows up!

4. <u>**A yielded life.**</u> Until I surrender to His plan for my life, and become obedient to the calling of His Spirit, I will not experience the blessings He has for me. Yielding is more than just coming to the church, sitting in the service, and listening to what the preacher says. Yielding occurs when we RESPOND to the call—surrender our wills in order to receive HIS. Many want to experience revival, but don't

want to leave their comfortable seats. They want to experience miracles, but don't want to let anyone lay hands upon them and pray.

You might say, "**Preacher!** *Are you saying that if I will do these four thing, THEN revival will come?*"
NO! If you will do these four things revival *IS ALREADY HERE*!

Chapter 14

What Shall I Write This Month?

Luke 10:41-42
Now as they went on their way, he entered a certain village, where a woman named Martha welcomed him into her home. She had a sister named Mary, who sat at the Lord's feet and listened to what he was saying.

But Martha was distracted by her many tasks; so she came to him and asked, "Lord, do you not care that my sister has left me to do all the work by myself? Tell her then to help me."

But the Lord answered her, "Martha, Martha, you are worried and distracted by many things; there is need of only one thing. {Other ancient authorities read [few things are necessary, or only one} Mary has chosen the better part, which will not be taken away from her." (NRSV)

Each month, I write an article for our church's newsletter. I try to be fresh and creative each month, but inspiration can sometimes be hard to find. As I contemplated a thought for one month's newsletter I struggled more than usual to come up with a fresh thought.

...Should I focus on the idea of missions and challenge the reader to greater awareness and involvement? After all, I would be going to Caracas, Venezuela at the beginning of the month. (Too obvious!)

...Should I direct reader's thoughts to an analysis of the events of Washington, D.C.? It would be a great teaching to those who fail or the techniques of splinter removal from the eye of another. (Way too obvious!)

...Maybe I could write about the changes in our lives as fall approaches—the weather, school activities, or even the time change would be great teaching points for dealing with the changes and challenges of life. (Over done!)

It seemed, the more I thought about it, the more distracted I became. That's when it hit me!

D-I-S-T-R-A-C-T-E-D!

That's it! How often do we set out to accomplish something and find ourselves thinking about something completely different? In fact, we might even start listing the distractions only to realize that we are yet again distracted by another thought.

Jesus knew there would be times of distraction in this life, but he also knew how important it was to remain focused on the task at hand. He said in Luke 9:62, "No one who puts his hand to the plow and looks back is fit for service in the kingdom of God." In other words, Christ is saying..."Don't let your service for the Lord be distracted by the thing behind or around you."

Jesus calmed a frustrated Martha in Luke 10:41 by saying "...you are worried about many things, but one thing is needed." He could say that to us much of the time. We find ourselves distracted by the "many things" and miss out on the most important thing.

The Distractions always come when we are trying to accomplish something great for God.

Peter was walking on the water when the wind and waves distracted him. It was when Peter lost his focus on the one thing that was important that he began to sink.

It happens to each of us in our walk with God. We are focused upon doing the will of God, and then the cares of life creep in.

...The bills and vacations distract us from obedient giving.
...Activities, trips and weekend recreation distract us from being in God's house.
...Personal fulfillment and needs distract us from ministering to the needs of others (wife, kids and church family).

Distractions will rob us from achieving God's blessings in our lives. The Apostle Paul said that he would not be distracted by the past, but would press on to the prize of the upward calling of God.

We would do well to listen to the instructions of God to His children in Joshua 1:7, "Be careful to obey all the law my servant Moses gave you, do not turn from it to the right or to the left, that you may be successful wherever you go." Stay focused upon what is important and do not allow yourself to be distracted from God's ways!

Chapter 15

Are You Da' Man?

Psalm 1
How blessed is the man who does not walk in the counsel of the wicked, nor stand in the path of sinners, nor sit in the seat of scoffers!

But his delight is in the law of the Lord, and in His law he meditates day and night.

And he will be like a tree firmly planted by streams of water, which yields its fruit in its season, and its leaf does not wither; and in whatever he does, he prospers.

The wicked are not so, but they are like chaff which the wind drives away.

Therefore the wicked will not stand in the judgment, nor sinners in the assembly of the righteous.

For the Lord knows the way of the righteous, but the way of the wicked will perish. (NAS)

Unless you've lived in a cave for the last several months, you've no doubt heard the expression, You Da' Man! It means that YOU have been recognized as having accomplished something great and are honored among all men or you have messed up really badly and you are getting the full blame!

Whatever the meaning, it generally means that an individual is set apart from the others around them. Look at the qualities it takes to be "Da' Man" who is blessed in all he does and ask yourself, "Are YOU Da' Man?"

Blessed is the man who...

1. Seeks Godly Counsel (v.1)

Proverbs 15:22 says, *"Plans will fail for lack of counsel, but with many advisors they succeed."*

This would surely apply to a man's unwillingness to stop and ask for directions when he is "disoriented," but it really goes deeper than that. It should be noted that you do not get "extra points" for doing it all yourself. It helps to seek spiritual advice when making decisions of any size.

2. Finds Godly Companionship (v. 1)

You will associate with people in the world, but the Scripture declares *"for though we are IN the world, we are not OF the world."*

Proverbs 13:20 says, *"He who walks with the wise grows wise, but a companion of fools suffers harm."*

Second Corinthians 6 warns us to not be *"unequally yoked"* together with unbelievers. Literally, we should not formulate partnerships with those who are unbelievers because we would be living according to two different systems.

3. Avoids A Critical Spirit (v .1)

Proverbs 21:23-24 says *"He who guards his mouth and his tongue keeps himself from calamity. The proud and arrogant man, "mocker" is his name; He behaves with overwhelming pride."* Just one chapter later (22:10) it says "drive out the mocker, and out goes the strife; quarrels and insults are ended."

A critical spirit divides a church and destroys the person. It sours and robs both the speaker and those who hear it of receiving God's best.

4. Delights In The Word Of God (v.2)

"On His law does he meditate day and night."

The Word of God must dwell in our hearts so we can make appropriate choices. Hebrews says that God's Word is powerful and sharper than any double-edged sword—and is a discerner of the thoughts and intents of the heart.

5. Strong and Steadfast (v. 3)

"He is like a tree planted by streams of living water." (Its roots are deep!) We can be strong and steadfast if our roots are deep in Christ. Colossians 2:6-7 says, *"so then, just as you received Christ Jesus as Lord, continue in him, rooted and built up in him, strengthened in the faith as you were taught and overflowing with thankfulness."*

Trees that are planted in streams are those that can stand in the midst of adversity—the storms of life!

6. He Is A Fruitful Man (v. 3)

"He yields his fruit in season." The fruits of Christianity are always in season.

John 15:8 says, *"This is to my fathers glory that you bear much fruit showing yourselves to be my disciples."* (v. 16) *"You did not choose me, but I chose you to go and bear fruit. Fruit that will last."*

Fruit is a sign of life!

7. His Testimony Is Consistent (v. 3)

"Whose leaf does not wither." This means that there is no change in his testimony. Regardless of the heat, drought or wind, this man's leaf doesn't wither.

Psalm 1 declares if you live this way—**"You Da' Man!"** You are blessed in all you do. You will prosper in every way.

Chapter 16

Give Me Liberty or GIVE ME DEATH!

Romans 6:16-23
Do you not know that when you present yourselves to someone as slaves for obedience, you are slaves of the one whom you obey, either of sin resulting in death, or of obedience resulting in righteousness?

But thanks be to God that though you were slaves of sin, you became obedient from the heart to that form of teaching to which you were committed, and having been freed from sin, you became slaves of righteousness.

I am speaking in human terms because of the weakness of your flesh. For just as you presented your members as slaves to impurity and to lawlessness, resulting in further lawlessness, so now present your members as slaves to righteousness, resulting in sanctification.

For when you were slaves of sin, you were free in regard to righteousness.

Therefore what benefit were you then deriving from the things of which you are now ashamed? For the outcome of those things is death.

But now having been freed from sin and enslaved to God, you derive your benefit, resulting in sanctification, and the outcome, eternal life. For the wages of sin is death, but the free gift of God is eternal life in Christ Jesus our Lord. (NAS)

As we celebrate Independence Day each year, my mind goes back to the days of the American Revolution. The birth of our nation began at a time when emotions ran deep. There was much frustration with the oppression of the British government.

They were bound by very restrictive regulations and extremely high taxes with no representation—or say in what went on.

Many felt as if they were about to strangle under the chokehold of the King of England.

They were entrenched with bondage and at the height of the frustration—with emotion running high—the colonists decided to REVOLT! They concluded that the bondage could not persist. They must break the hold.

It was during a very heated discussion of the issues and problems they faced that Patrick Henry stood up and spouted the words "Give me liberty or give me death!"

It seems he felt in order to go on living, he must have Liberty. This great American couldn't have been closer to the truth.

Our text confirms that as human beings we must be free from sin (the bondage of Satan himself) or we WILL DIE!

"The wages or result of sin is death!"

Contrastly, if we accept the Liberty/Freedom from sin offered through Christ, the gift—the benefit—is eternal life!

"Give me Liberty or Give me Death!"

Many in our world are slaves to sin and to Satan. People find themselves bound by addiction, defeat and the lusts of the flesh. Unless there is liberty—there will be death!

We must be free. How can we find liberty/freedom? According to 2 Corinthians 3:17 it says, *"The Lord is the Spirit, and where the Spirit of the Lord is, there is liberty."*

Romans 6:22 says, *"But now that you have been set free from sin and have become slaves to God, the benefit you reap leads to holiness and the result is eternal life."* On this basis, you can conclude: Where the Spirit is, there is liberty. Where there is liberty, there is life. We must have liberty or we will find death!

Why is it so important to be free?

IF we could talk to the slaves of the 1800s who were treated as possessions—bought and sold—beaten and chained, maybe we could get an idea of how important freedom is.

IF we could sit face to face with the Jews held in the concentration camps of Germany and find out what it was like to smell the smell of death, what it was like to hear the screams of those tortured, maybe then we could get an idea of how important freedom is.

IF we could talk to the demonic who roamed the tombs in Luke 8 and hear his story of his maiming, his chains and torment by Satan's demons, and if we could talk to him after Jesus delivered him, maybe we could understand the importance of freedom.

Many are bound today. They are imprisoned by fear...chained by guilt...oppressed by the lies of Satan.

Slaves to Satan—slaves to sin. They need freedom. They cry out, "Give me freedom or I will die."

My Bible tells me that where the Spirit of the Lord is, there is liberty—*liberty from sin...liberty from guilt...liberty from addiction to lust.*

It is the freedom from the condemnation and the dominion of Satan.

If you long for liberty as they did in the days of the American Revolution, you need only to pray and ask for Christ to come into your life and set you free from your bondage. The scripture declares, *"Whom the Son (Jesus) sets free is free indeed."*

As you celebrate your next Independence Day remember the spiritual liberty you have in Christ!

Chapter 17

Back To School Issue

Deuteronomy 5:1
Then Moses summoned all Israel, and said to them, "Hear, O Israel, the statutes and the ordinances which I am speaking today in your hearing, that you may learn them and observe them carefully. (NAS)

Deuteronomy 6:1-3
"Now this is the commandment, the statutes and the judgments which the Lord your God has commanded me to teach you, that you might do them in the land where you are going over to possess it, so that you and your son and your grandson might fear the Lord your God, to keep all His statutes and His commandments, which I command you, all the days of your life, and that your days may be prolonged.

"O Israel, you should listen and be careful to do it, that it may be well with you and that you may multiply greatly, just as the Lord, the God of your fathers, has promised you, in a land flowing with milk and honey. (NAS)

As the fall approaches, the return to school marks the end of summer for kids and parents alike. Our family routine becomes steadier and our thoughts are directed to the process of learning.

Throughout God's Word we are commanded to commit ourselves to learning. The words LEARN, LEARNED, and LEARNING appears 62 times in the Old and New Testament. It is an important topic for us to consider.

You see, learning is not only for kids. Each of us must learn everyday. My 8th grade English teacher had a poster on his wall that said, *"When you're through learning, you're through!"* It is a true statement. We are learning from the moment we begin living until the moment we stop.

The idea of **"Going Back to School"** will get a mixed response from kids and adults, but in reality we have no choice in the matter. Learning is a part of living.

In Deuteronomy 5:1, Moses summoned the Israelites to hear and learn the decrees and laws of God. The covenant of God was based upon their obedience to His mandates and if they failed to learn them, they would surely fail. Throughout the entire book of Deuteronomy, Moses urged them to learn His ways and to learn to fear God.

As children of God, we must go "back to school" and learn His ways. One author wrote that learning involves three essential aspects...knowing, being and doing!

Knowing God is essential to the learning process. When we study the facts and details about a subject we become knowledgeable. That is to say that we become familiar with the subject and its special qualities.

What we know almost always brings about changes in who we are **_being_**. Our character is molded by what we know. We learn by our mistakes and make adjustments in our lives.

The learning process must then take the third step into the area of **_doing_**! If we **KNOW** something, **AND** we allow what we know to become part of our **BEING—then** it will show in our **DOING!** Our actions are a direct result of the learning process.

It's time for all of us to go "back to school" to submit ourselves to the learning process again and become the people God desires us to be.

Hebrews 5:12-6:2 says, *"For though by this time you ought to be teachers, you have need again for someone to teach you the elementary principles of the oracles of God, and you have come to need milk and not solid food.*

"For everyone who partakes only of milk is not accustomed to the word of righteousness, for he is a babe. But solid food is for the mature, who because of practice have their senses trained to discern good and evil.

"Therefore leaving the elementary teaching about the Christ, let us press on to maturity, not laying again a foundation of repentance from dead works and of faith toward God, of instruction about washings, and laying on of hands, and the resurrection of the dead, and eternal judgment."

Chapter 18

Putting The '<u>REAL</u>' in Religion!

James 1:27
If anyone thinks himself to be religious, and yet does not bridle his tongue but deceives his own heart, this man's religion is worthless.
This is pure and undefiled religion in the sight of our God and Father, to visit orphans and widows in their distress, and to keep oneself unstained by the world. (NAS)

The word religion has little meaning in today's society. People have planned the church out of their lives in most respects and all that remains is a place of forms, rituals and traditions. People become so full of their religion, they soon lose sight of the reason they do things—or for WHOM they do them.

The church has allowed religion to become lifeless and dysfunctional because they have lost focus of what is REAL.

Can we make religion real again? Look at James 1:7 for a look at what real religion is. Simply paraphrased, <u>Religion that is acceptable by God is to look after widows and orphans—and to keep oneself from being polluted</u>. Sounds basic enough. In its simplest form—religion should be about 1) social concern and 2) holy conduct.

Social Concern: "to visit the orphans and widows in their distress." This doesn't mean that we just stop by and say "hi." The word visit here means that we enter the scene and actually become a part of the scene. In other words, we must come into the midst of their trouble and minister to them.

Somehow the church has backed away from the responsibility of taking care of the needy. We have developed the same mentality as the world—*"the government will take care of them."* Scripture doesn't allow us to depend upon the world's system to do the work we have been called to do. The reason the government has so much say in our society is because we have developed a dependence upon it for basic provision. I remember a day in our country when people depended upon the church in that way. The church also had great influence in the community. That is no longer the case! We lost our influence when we failed to care about the REAL needs of people.

We can no longer expect the world to do our jobs. We must get involved in ministering to the needy around us. The church is mostly irrelevant in the lives of people today because they feel it no longer cares. Maybe you've heard, *"People will never care how much we know, until they know how much we care."* I don't know who originated the statement, but it is very true.

Holy Conduct: We haven't done very well in this area either. We've become so much like the world that people do not see the difference any more. We must return to holiness.

Holiness is not just a matter of **NOT** doing unholy things—but rather, being changed inside out so that we are different. It is time we stop talking about how others should live and start living the way WE should live. The church has pointed fingers at others but failed to live out what it preaches. The world has tuned the church out and labeled it extremists and intolerant of others because it (the world) has seen the inconsistency and emptiness of its words and conduct. This must change.

How can we do these things and show God to the world around us? Well, the answer is found in the first line of our text—"Father." This word speaks of relationship—which is what the world lacks with its creator. If we can minister the love of God through our relationships, we can establish a connection with those around us.

We must minister to the widows and orphans by showing the love of the "Father" to them. They don't need forms or rituals—they need the Father!

Chapter 19

There's Just "Something" About That Psalm!

Psalm 46:8-11
Come, behold the works of the Lord, Who has wrought desolations in the earth. He makes wars to cease to the end of the earth; He breaks the bow and cuts the spear in two; He burns the chariots with fire.

"Cease striving and know that I am God; I will be exalted among the nations, I will be exalted in the earth."

The Lord of hosts is with us; The God of Jacob is our stronghold. Selah. (NAS)

Have you ever been hungry for "something," but you just didn't know what it was? There are nights when I've looked in the refrigerator, the cabinets, the pantry—and then started over. I think we can all remember looking at a restaurant menu or wandering through a convenience mart looking for that one "something" that will satisfy our inner cravings.

There are many people today looking for "something" to fill the spiritual emptiness in their lives in much the same way. I've found that "something" in Psalm 46.

SOMETHING TO SEE! (v. 8)
Come and see the works of God. (NIV) The word "behold" is used in the King James Version and means to look and consider—not just glance.

God created us with sight so that we could behold His beauty. He gave such care to the detail of creation and meant for it to be seen, not just glanced at. There really are "purple mountains" and "amber waves of grain."

In Isaiah 6:1, the prophet tells us, *"I saw [beheld] the Lord."* This was no mere glance, but an awe-inspired gaze into the beauty and holiness of God. To paraphrase Paul's declaration in Philippians 2:10, "Every knee shall bow, and every JAW will DROP!"

"Come and see the works of God." See His glory fill the temple, His grace to redeem mankind, His faithfulness to His people—*AND* His judgement upon ungodliness.

SOMETHING TO BE! (v. 10)

"...be still..." This is a tall order for today's culture. We seem to think that we must be constantly "doing," but God desires that we BE still.

Educators will tell you that learning cannot take place effectively until we are still. Teachers do not allow commotion, running or jabbering in the classroom. They take great strides to keep things quiet so that learning can take place.

We live in a world of distractions. God says, BE STILL! He longs for us to be quieted in His presence so that we can listen to His counsel.

Jonathan Edwards said, "We must be still as to words and as to actions so as not to oppose God." When we protest, complain and defy God's wisdom in our lives, we are opposing Him.

SOMETHING TO KNOW! (v. 10)

"...and know [recognize and understand] that I am God." Knowledge is important to our lives. Without knowledge, we cannot advance in our careers. Without knowledge, we are doomed to stay in ignorance. God desires that we KNOW him.

In order to know Him, we must spend time with Him. As we learn His ways and listen to His voice, we will come to KNOW Him. If we KNOW that He is God, then we will have hope, peace and joy for the days ahead of us.

SOMETHING TO BELIEVE! (v. 11)

"The Lord of hosts is with us; the God of Jacob is our refuge..." This is a repeat of verse 7. Anytime you see something repeated in Scripture, it is an indication of its importance to us.

God wants us to BELIEVE in Him for our safety and protection. We are NOT alone! Verses 1 through 3 remind us that there is no reason to be afraid because he is "a very present and well-proved help in trouble."

Are you searching for "something?" God gives us "something" ...To SEE ...To BE ...To KNOW... and To BELIEVE! Just like the old saying—"Seeing is believing!" SEEING Him helps us to BE Still, so that we can KNOW Him and BELIEVE in Him!

Chapter 20

Faith That Works!

Hebrews 10:35-36
Therefore, do not throw away your confidence, which has a great reward. For you have need of endurance, so that when you have done the will of God, you may receive what was promised. (NAS)

I'm sure at one time or another we have all struggled with the idea of faith and how it works. There have been times in all of our lives that we did not see the results we were looking for and began to question our faith. In those moments, we feel that our faith must have been defective because it didn't work. We must have a **Faith That Works!**

You might expect me to lead you to James chapter 2 where it tells about faith without works being dead. Simply put, faith that is not accompanied by works is a faith that doesn't work—a dead faith—and without faith it is impossible to please God. While all of this is true, I encourage you to look to Hebrews 10 to see what a *"Faith That Works"* is. What does a "Faith That Works" do?

Faith Confides! Verse 35 of Hebrews 10 tells us not to throw away our confidence. Confidence is a trust and assurance that brings comfort and rest in God and His ability to work on our behalf. Too often we are quick to throw away our confidence because our confidence is in the wrong things. Simply put, if the one you are confiding in is greater than what you are up against you will remain confident. If not, you will become intimidated and lose heart. The Bible says, "Some trust in chariots...but we trust in the name of the Lord our God!"

Faith Perseveres! Verse 36 says, "you have need of endurance." This is no easy road! The things we are attempting to achieve are contrary to the flesh and the god of this world (Satan). Do not lose heart! God has overcome the world.

Our faith is not a sprint, but a marathon. Marathon runners are some of the most physically fit people there are, because they condition themselves to complete the race. No one enters the race thinking, *"If I can just make it the first lap I'll be satisfied."* NO! They persevere in training so that they can endure and finish the race.

Galatians 6:9 reminds us not to become weary in doing good. We will reap a harvest if we don't give up!

Faith Obeys! Verse 36 continues to say. "...after you have DONE the will of God." That phrase is written in the past tense indicating that it is a completed task. A *Faith That Works* demands that we be obedient EVERY DAY! We cannot selectively obey and expect God to fulfill His part of the promise.

Faith Receives! We can expect to receive the promise AFTER we have DONE the will of God! All that God has promised is ours. The same God who created the universe and raised Christ will also make you victorious. Verse 38 says, "My righteous ones will LIVE by faith." When we make faith a way of life, we can live in the promises of God.

If our faith is CONFIDING, PERSEVERING and OBEYING—we will be RECEIVING. That is a Faith That Works! In its simplest form, a "Faith That Works" is one that is productive in all of these ways.

Chapter 21

What To Do When God Is Late!

James 1:2-7, 12, 19, 22

"Consider it pure joy, my brothers, when ever you face trials of many kinds, because you know that the testing of your faith develops perseverance. Perseverance must finish its work so that you may be mature and complete, not lacking anything. If any of you lacks wisdom, he should ask God, who gives generously to all without finding fault, and it will be given to him, but when he asks, he must believe and not doubt, because he who doubts is like a wave of the sea, blown and tossed by the wind. That man should not think he would receive anything from the Lord. Blessed is the man, who perseveres under trial, because when he has stood the test, he will receive the crown of life that God has promised to those who love him. My dear brothers, take note of this. Everyone should be quick to listen, slow to speak and slow to become angry. Do not merely listen to the word, and so deceive yourselves. Do what it says." (NIV)

In today's world of instant cameras, microwaves, 10-minute oil changes and express mail, we have grown weary of waiting for answers. Our lives in God are no different. We seem to function with the mind-set that if the answer doesn't come when we want it—God is late!

Where is the problem? Is it with God or **with us?** According to *my* Bible, God's timing is perfect. Galatians 4:4 speaks of God sending His Son at the "fullness of time"—or—at the precise time! God has a time schedule, but it is **not** like ours. We want things to happen by *our* watches.

A student asked a college president, "Can I take a shorter course of study than the one prescribed?"

"Oh yes!" the president replied. "But it all depends on what you want to be. When God wants to make a giant oak, He takes many years. But when He wants to make a squash, He takes a few months!"

We must understand that God knows what's best. Verse 4 of our text says, "so that you many be mature and complete, not lacking anything!"

We read the scriptures and see the fire fall, the sea split, and the dead raised and we demand action ***now***. When we don't see the answer right away—we feel forsaken. The word "wait" is not a pleasant one for us to hear, but it appears 34 times in scripture. At least 30 of those are specifically ***"waiting upon God."***

Isaiah 30:18 says, "Blessed are they that wait." Lamentations 3:25 says "The Lord is good to them that wait for Him."

So—what do you do when God is "late?" ***Wait!*** That does ***not*** mean that you do nothing. Our text gives us some things that we can do while waiting.

1. **Consider It Joy! (v. 2-4)** God is working on something special. Through each experience, we have the opportunity to grow and mature into the person God desires us to be.

2. **Ask…God! (v .5)** Ephesians 3:20 says that He is able to do exceedingly and abundantly above all we can ask for or think. When we make our requests known to Him through praise and thanksgiving, His transcendent peace will come upon us. Our text says if you lack wisdom ***ask God***. If you're unsure of what the next step is you need wisdom so that you don't make the wrong choice.

3. **Believe and NOT Doubt (v. 6)** The text says a double-minded man is unstable in all his ways. If you come with a "maybe" mentality, don't think you're going to receive what you're asking for. Come in ***faith believing.***

4. **Persevere Under Trial (v. 12).** When you stand the test, you will receive a crown. Galatians 6:9 says not to become weary in doing good. But that we would reap a harvest if we didn't give up.

5. **Quick To Listen & Slow To Speak (v. 19)** God can't speak if you're talking. Even more than that—power of

life and death are in the tongue. If you don't watch what you say—your words can snare you.

6. **Don't Just Listen But Do What The Word Says (v. 22)** Verse 25 says that a man that does the Word "will be blessed in what he does."

If you will follow these instructions "when God is late," I dare say that the waiting will not seem that long.

Chapter 22

Tossing Our Caps Over The Wall

Philippians 3:7-14
But whatever things were gain to me, those things I have counted as loss for the sake of Christ. More than that, I count all things to be loss in view of the surpassing value of knowing Christ Jesus my Lord, for whom I have suffered the loss of all things, and count them but rubbish in order that I may gain Christ, and may be found in Him, not having a righteousness of my own derived from the Law, but that which is through faith in Christ, the righteousness which comes from God on the basis of faith that I may know Him, and the power of His resurrection and the fellowship of His sufferings, being conformed to His death; in order that I may attain to the resurrection from the dead.

Not that I have already obtained it, or have already become perfect, but I press on in order that I may lay hold of that for which also I was laid hold of by Christ Jesus.

Brethren, I do not regard myself as having laid hold of it yet; but one thing I do: forgetting what lies behind and reaching forward to what lies ahead, I press on toward the goal for the prize of the upward call of God in Christ Jesus. (NAS)

Frank O'Conner, a well-known American author, wrote of his boyhood, and he shared the story of him and his friend taking journeys in the countryside each day in the summer. They would wander through the hills and valleys of his family's orchard. Each day at a certain point in their journey, they would reach the orchard wall. The wall was so tall and so impossible looking that they would sit and think about how they would scale it, and each day they would determine that it was impossible and go back home.

One day they wandered as they always had and came to the wall as usual. But this day would be different. Instead of sitting down, thinking about it, and giving up—they took off their caps and threw them over the wall. Giving themselves no other alternative but to follow them.

I love that story! I can think of no better illustration of where each of us are today than these boys at the wall.

The wall to these boys was no different than the River Jordan was to the children of Israel. It was the obstacle to progress and blessing.

There will always be obstacles that must be overcome in order to receive the blessing God has prepared.

The enemy wants nothing more than to see you defeated and discouraged. He used the Red Sea with Moses, the walls of Jericho with Joshua, the Midianites with Gideon and Goliath with David. Each of these obstacles looked too big— too difficult and impossible. I'm glad that God is not hindered by Satan's obstacles.

I read where the Red Sea was split in two, the walls of Jericho tumbled down and every man went straight in, the Midianites were so afraid that they killed each other, and Goliath "laid down" with a horrible headache.

Each of these men encountered a wall, but through their faith and trust in God, they scaled that wall to achieve victory.

Victory cannot be achieved by sitting at the foot of the wall and thinking about it! Victory will only take place if we scale it.

It is not going to be an easy task. The wall represents the outer limits of our past experience. Beyond the wall are uncharted territories and new experiences. We are filled with wonder and anticipation of what is ahead in each new day. The wall looks tall and impossible to scale.

We begin asking ourselves, "Can my life be different?" or "What must I change?" and "What will those changes cost me?" We must ask ourselves those questions, but we must also trust God for the answers. If we try to figure it all out in advance, we will never advance.

My encouragement to you for each day of opportunity and blessing is to **"*Toss Your Cap Over The Wall!*"** **Then follow it!**

Chapter 23

Reason To Rejoice!

Luke 10:17-20
And the seventy returned with joy, saying, "Lord, even the demons are subject to us in Your name."

And He said to them, "I was watching Satan fall from heaven like lightning.

"Behold, I have given you authority to tread upon serpents and scorpions, and over all the power of the enemy, and nothing shall injure you.

"Nevertheless do not rejoice in this, that the spirits are subject to you, but rejoice that your names are recorded in heaven." (NAS)

These insightful words in Luke 10:20 are very timely as we have now entered the 21st century. I believe the church world is in danger of falling victim to the "pendulum effect." For a period of time in Christian experience the power and authority within the believer through Christ was avoided or ignored, but in recent years it seems the pendulum has swung in reverse direction—almost to the neglect of the personal relationship with Christ.

Lest you surmise that I am teaching that the power of God in the believer is unimportant, let me point out that the purpose of Pentecost was to empower the church (Acts 1:8), but listen to Christ's words...

If you want to rejoice about something—rejoice that your name is written in the Book of Life, not that demons are subject to you.

Society today seems obsessed with power. People are willing to do anything to ride to the top—all for the sake of power. History has shown that people are drawn to powerful individuals. Examples include Hitler, Jim Jones, and more recently David Koresh. Those who followed them were drawn by power that caused them to abandon their personal convictions.

Power pursued or gained for a selfish motive is destructive not only to self, but also to those associated with it. I believe that is why Christ said what He did in Luke 10:20. He basically said, *"The basis for rejoicing is not in the power you possess, but in the relationship that brings you that power."* The reality is that we have no real power except through Christ. Jesus spoke these words in John 15:5, *"If a man remains in Me and I in him, he will bear much fruit; apart from Me you can do nothing."*

Having power in this life is great, but of what eternal consequence is power if we miss heaven? *"What good will it be for a man if he gains the whole world, yet forfeits his soul?"* (Mt. 16:26 NIV)

Our basis for rejoicing must be making sure that our names are in that Book. The power will come as a direct result of our growing relationship with Christ!

Chapter 24

The Spirit Of Eleazer

1 Chronicles 11:10-14
Now these are the heads of the mighty men whom David had, who gave him strong support in his kingdom, together with all Israel, to make him king, according to the word of the Lord concerning Israel.

And these constitute the list of the mighty men whom David had: Jashobeam, the son of a Hachmonite, the chief of the thirty; he lifted up his spear against three hundred whom he killed at one time.

And after him was Eleazar the son of Dodo, the Ahohite, who was one of the three mighty men. He was with David at Pasdammim when the Philistines were gathered together there to battle, and there was a plot of ground full of barley; and the people fled before the Philistines. And they took their stand in the midst of the plot, and defended it, and struck down the Philistines; and the Lord saved them by a great victory. (NAS)

2 Samuel 23:9-10
...and after him was Eleazar the son of Dodo the Ahohite, one of the three mighty men with David when they defied the Philistines who were gathered there to battle and the men of Israel had withdrawn.

He arose and struck the Philistines until his hand was weary and clung to the sword, and the Lord brought about a great victory that day; and the people returned after him only to strip the slain. (NAS)

"Behind every successful political leader is a successful campaign advisor." I realize this is a re-tooling of the well-known quote, but let's face it—political leaders do not become political leaders without the help of some aggressive management and advice that propels them into the forefront of the voter's thinking. The election is won through the hard work of staffers who work the trenches, back rooms and town halls. They are the ones who often do the "dirty work" of the attack and get the "bloodiest" in the battle.

It is no different today from the past. In fact, the best illustration of this fact is found in the life of David—the second political leader of Israel.

We find him in 1 Chronicles 11 being finally made king nearly twenty years after being anointed. His predecessor fought hard to retain office. We find that David's most recent years were a struggle to stay alive amidst the vicious pursuit of King Saul.

It was during this time, that David formed some very important friendships with men who would become his closest advisors and supporters. They were instrumental in keeping him alive in the battles leading up to this "crowning moment."

The Bible goes on to record that these "mighty men," as they were called, continued to work in David's behalf to extend the borders of his kingdom to the extent of God's promise. They worked the trenches of the battle to win the ultimate victory for their leader.

One of these "mighty men" was Eleazer. He was one of the elite of David's operatives in the establishment of his kingdom. Eleazer had a unique spirit about him that David needed to accomplish his goal. The Scripture records that he "stood his ground and struck down the Philistines till his hand grew tired and froze to the sword." (2 Samuel 23:10)

This verse goes on to say, "The Lord brought about a great victory that day; and the people returned after him only to plunder." In other words, they only had to come back to pick up the stuff left by the defeated army.

This seems like a far cry from the workers in most churches. Many stay in the fray of battle until it gets tough, then they bow out. Eleazer's hand stuck to the sword and he couldn't let go. How many of today's Christians leave at the first sight of tension—let alone blood shed?

God desires to have some "mighty men and women" who will catch the spirit of Eleazer to advance the borders of the Kingdom of God.

How do we catch the spirit of Eleazer?

Put Your Hand To The Sword! The battle cannot be fought unless some warriors put their hand to the sword. We must accept the challenge and commit ourselves to establishing the Kingdom of our leader, who is not a politician or political leader, but Jesus Christ Himself!

The nation of Israel stood with David in 1 Chronicles 11 and made him their king. Today, our Lord is looking for a church who will take up the sword and make him the king of their lives.

Stand Your Ground! We cannot back down in the face of battle. We MUST stay put. 1 Chronicles 11:14-15 tells us of when the Philistines advanced on a piece of ground full of barley, but the mighty men—of which Eleazer was one—stationed themselves in the middle of the field, defended it, and killed the Philistines.

Never Let Go! Our text says, "His hand stuck to the sword." He may have wanted to let go in the midst of his battle, but he couldn't. I have often visualized him almost trying to shake the sword from his hand to let go and killing a few dozen more.

We need this kind of mighty men and women in our churches today. People who will put their hands to the sword, stand their ground and never let go—in the spirit of Eleazer!

The Kingdom is counting on you!

Chapter 25

Do We Need FORM-al Religion?

1 Timothy 3:1-5
But realize this, that in the last days difficult times will come.
For men will be lovers of self, lovers of money, boastful, arrogant, revilers, disobedient to parents, ungrateful, unholy, unloving, irreconcilable, malicious gossips, without self-control, brutal, haters of good, treacherous, reckless, conceited, lovers of pleasure rather than lovers of God; holding to a form of godliness, although they have denied its power; and avoid such men as these.
(NAS)

Not long ago, our nation was in a frenzy concerning comments by a certain northern governor about the value of "organized religion." Talk show hosts and news columnists "wrestled" and debated the issue from every angle...except the <u>spiritual</u> one.

I must admit, as a pastor, my initial response was one of anger, disgust and piety. I was even a bit shocked to see that liberal members of the media had a similar response to mine. As I continued to reflect on the statement, however, the true weight of the whole issue began to settle in my spirit. It finally dawned on me that this was a spiritual commentary upon our nation and the church itself.

What About America?
Consider the irony of the number of liberal, ungodly and immoral people outraged by this politician's statement. These are the same people who are normally defending the "choice" of abortion, gay rights and bashing the "religious right." It seems hypocritical that they would condemn such a statement. It is almost as if they consider themselves one of us!

Read 2 Timothy 3:1-5 and I think you'll see it for what it really is. It is a "form" of godliness with a denial of power. It seems apparent that America still considers itself a Christian nation. That is nothing more than a "FORM-al" religion.

The term "form of godliness" refers to any one of the following: an appearance, a shadow, a hint, a glimmer or resemblance. Do these terms refer to America's godliness? Sadly, the answer is "Yes!"

This should not surprise us! Americans are great at the charade of success in the midst of failure. We have an "appearance" of godliness. Politicians find it "appealing" to attend church in the eyes of the camera. Candidates who pound podiums and quote Scriptures often get votes, but after elected their core values are displayed at the expense of our national morality. That kind of "FORM-al" religion we DON'T need.

But wait! It goes even deeper than this.

What About The Church?

You might be tempted to read the passage of Scripture mentioned above and think that it only refers to the world. But if you do, you would be mistaken. As the days advance toward the coming of the Lord, we are seeing Paul's descriptions of behavior in the last days creeping into the church. As I read the list of carnal activities I'm ashamed to admit that I have dealt with many of these in my own pastorates. Paul even warns of those who are always learning, but are never able to acknowledge the truth. Could we have ever imagined a time when pastors would be opposed for preaching the truth of Scripture concerning sin and Godliness and instead being urged to be more soothing and uplifting with their messages?

We must consider the effects of such behavior upon the world around us. People often form opinions based upon what they have seen or experienced personally. Is it possible that this governor was commenting on the basis of some of the churches and Christians he has personally dealt with? Is it possible that he, and those who feel as he does, have witnessed the lack of consistency, the "form" of godliness and lack of power in the church and its members?

If it is possible, we who profess Christianity should wake up, stop pointing fingers and being critical of those who oppose us. We have often given them no cause to think or feel differently.

I believe that if this governor had ever been faced with Christians who had more than a FORM of godliness—people who lived in the power and love of God—his statement would have been much different.

We must ask ourselves, "What have we given this world to look at?" If we were honest in our response to the question, we would have to admit that it has been nothing more than lifeless, "FORM-al" religion! No wonder they live with an appearance of godliness but deny that anything else exists. It is all they have ever seen in us.

In the final analysis, people cannot deny what they have seen with their own eyes. Therefore, we must allow God's power and love to be displayed in and through us in order to reach them with our message.

Chapter 26

Hope In The Valley

Acts 16:22-30

And the crowd rose up together against them, and the chief magistrates tore their robes off them, and proceeded to order them to be beaten with rods.

And when they had inflicted many blows upon them, they threw them into prison, commanding the jailer to guard them securely; and he, having received such a command, threw them into the inner prison, and fastened their feet in the stocks.

But about midnight Paul and Silas were praying and singing hymns of praise to God, and the prisoners were listening to them; and suddenly there came a great earthquake, so that the foundations of the prison house were shaken; and immediately all the doors were opened, and everyone's chains were unfastened.

And when the jailer had been roused out of sleep and had seen the prison doors opened, he drew his sword and was about to kill himself, supposing that the prisoners had escaped.

But Paul cried out with a loud voice, saying, "Do yourself no harm, for we are all here!"

And he called for lights and rushed in and, trembling with fear, he fell down before Paul and Silas, and after he brought them out, he said, "Sirs, what must I do to be saved?" (NAS)

You have no doubt had days in your life when it seemed nothing could go wrong. Days when the victory seems so sweet it could last forever. But there were also days when everything falls apart—"Murphy's Law" kind of days. Like the day you wake up in the hospital and your insurance agent tells you that your policy covers falling off the roof, but not hitting the ground. Valley days! We would just as soon not repeat them or even go through them at all, but they're inevitable. The valley days come. Even in Bible hero's lives.

In Acts 16 we see a day in the lives of Paul and Silas. They had been experiencing one victory after another. The church was strengthened (v. 5), Lydia and her family had found Christ (v.14), and a demon possessed slave girl was delivered (v. 16-18). They had reached the peak of the mountain and then came the valley.

It was quickly apparent that the owners of the fortune-telling slave girl were not happy that their moneymaker had lost her ability, so they had our heroes beaten and thrown in jail.

They went from the mountain top to being beaten, humiliated and imprisoned. But their day wasn't over. As they sat in stocks in the maximum security cell an earthquake occurred and the jail almost caved in on top of them. Talk about a bad day!

We would be tempted to say "Paul and Silas, you must be out of God's will! Maybe you have sin in your lives. You had better get used to pin-striped PJ's."

It might have been enough to discourage most folks, but not Paul and Silas. At about midnight they started singing. I've often imagined what they sang. *Nearer My God To Thee? Hold The Fort? Or I Shall Not Be Moved?* NO! I'm not sure what they started with, but I'm almost positive that it ended with *"He Set Me Free"* because as they started that first verse that says "Once like a bird in prison I dwelt..." the jail started to shake, rattle and roll.

You thought Elvis invented the *"Jail House Rock,"* but now you know that it was God Almighty Himself. You see, in the midst of the valley, He sent His Spirit through the victory won by the Solid Rock and loosened everyone's chains. The Jailer, ready to take his own life at the loss of his prisoners, noticed that these two singing jail birds hadn't escaped. Amazed at their testimony, he asked, "What must I do to be saved?"

If Paul and Silas had allowed themselves to be bitter or angry—or if they had been complaining or feeling sorry for themselves, do you think the Jailer would have been won to Christ?

We must allow the hope of God to flow into our valley experiences so that He will be glorified in ALL circumstances. Paul and Silas had peace and joy in the midst of their valley and soon they had victory too!

Philippians 4 says "Be anxious for nothing, but in everything, by prayer and supplication make your request made known unto God…and the peace of God that passes all understanding will guard your hearts and minds through Christ Jesus."

When the valleys come—sing praise to the Lord—there is hope!

Chapter 27

My Jesus, My Savior!

Luke 2:11
　And in the same region there were some shepherds staying out in the fields, and keeping watch over their flock by night.
　And an angel of the Lord suddenly stood before them, and the glory of the Lord shone around them; and they were terribly frightened.
　And the angel said to them, "Do not be afraid; for behold, I bring you good news of a great joy which shall be for all the people; for today in the city of David there has been born for you a Savior, who is Christ the Lord. (NAS)

With the onset of spring, our world gives attention to the new life that "springs" forth around us. It is a special time of year with great spiritual significance as we consider the "new life" brought to mankind at the death, burial and resurrection of Jesus Christ.

Luke 2:11 says, "For there is born to you this day in the city of David a savior, who is Christ the Lord." Which literally means, "your savior is born and He is the Messiah!"

The Savior/Messiah had been prophecied for many centuries. All of Israel anticipated His birth because he would surely deliver them from the oppression of the Roman government. But in typical fashion, they missed it because they figured it would be different. They were looking for a political and military savior, but what they got was a spiritual one.

In fact, there were times in Christ's ministry that he could have been made king by force and lead a revolt. This kingdom would be different, however. The spiritual revolt that He would bring about would have eternal consequences.

Luke 19:10 says that Christ "came to seek and to SAVE that which was lost." John 3:17 said that He didn't come to condemn the world, but that the world might be SAVED through Him. 1 Timothy 1:15 says, "Christ Jesus came into the world to SAVE sinners."

My Savior Was My Substitute!
He Went To The Cross For Me.

Isaiah 53:5 declares, "He was wounded for our (my) transgressions. He was bruised for our (my) iniquities." Galatians 3:18 says, "Christ redeemed us from the curse of the law by becoming a curse for us." Peter described it in 1 Peter 3:18 as the righteous being given for the unrighteous.

Literally, the Man who knew no sin BECAME sin for us by being our (my) substitute.

My Savior Was My Sacrifice!
He Went To The Grave For Me.

Not only did he take my place by going to the cross, but he paid the price by going to the grave.

My sin demanded death, so Christ became my sacrifice. "He gave himself up for us as a fragrant offering and sacrifice to God." (Ephesians 5:2) No one else was worthy to pay that price because it demanded a lamb that was without spot or blemish, so He became the sacrifice because He was without sin!

"This is how we know what love is: Jesus Christ laid down his life for us." (1 Jn. 3:16)

My Savior Was My Supplier!
He Went To The Father For Me.

According to the Word of God, Christ went to the Father to send the Holy Spirit as a teacher and comforter. He went to the father to prepare a place for us. (John 14) And He went to the Father to make intercession for us. (Heb. 7:25)

He literally became the supplier of my every need. That would not have been possible without His resurrection and ascension into heaven.

The Savior became my **Substitute**—
    He went to the Cross for Me!
The Savior became my **Sacrifice**—
    He went to the Grave for Me!
The Savior became my **Supplier**—

He went to the <u>Father</u> for Me!

OH, What A Savior!

Chapter 28

The Sacrifice Of Praise

Hebrews 13:5
Through Him then, let us continually offer up a sacrifice of praise to God, that is, the fruit of lips that give thanks to His name. (NAS)

Having grown up in church since my earliest remembrance I have often heard the Sacrifice of Praise defined as "praising the Lord even when you don't feel like it." While I feel it is important to praise the Lord regardless of whether you feel like it or not, I doubt that giving the Lord something we don't feel is really an acceptable sacrifice. I believe that the Scripture is indicating something more than a half-hearted attempt at giving the Lord praise.

When Old Testament "believers" made a sacrifice to the Lord it was not because they didn't feel like it. Something given unwillingly was not really considered a sacrifice. The New Testament teaches that nothing should be given reluctantly, under compulsion or unwillingly, for the Lord loves a cheerful giver.

The word sacrifice comes from the Greek word that means to "kill or slaughter for a purpose." Jack Hayford says, *"Praise often requires that we 'kill' our pride, fear, or sloth—anything that threatens to diminish or interfere with our worship of the Lord."*

The verse above says, "Through Jesus, let us offer...." Our sacrifice should be no less willing or complete as Christ's. Romans 12:1 says that we should offer our bodies a living sacrifice...which is our reasonable service. It is <u>*the least*</u> we can do.

When we combine the idea of sacrifice with the concept of praise it is important to understand that for the Christian, praise is a natural product of lips that confess his name. In light of these things we must understand three important aspects of praise.

1. The PURPOSE Of Praise!

Praise builds my relationship with God. Psalm 22:3 says that He is enthroned in the praises of Israel. This means that He inhabits, dwells and abides in the praises of His people. The word "inhabit" means *"to sit down, to remain, to settle or to marry."*

In other words, God doesn't just visit when we praise Him, but His presence abides with us.

You could actually say that praise brings the presence of God into my daily life—my day to day experience. When I'm alone, discouraged or feel deserted I can praise Him and He will abide with me. He literally gets involved in my life, and when God gets involved with something, things change!

2. The PRACTICS Of Praise!

David gives us the example of being an effective worshipper of God in Psalm 63:1-4.

A) God, you are MY God. He established relationship.

B) Earnestly (early) I seek you. He re-arranged priorities.

C) My soul longs for you. He developed an intense desire.

D) I have seen you in the sanctuary. He worshipped with God's people.

E) Your loving kindness is better than life. He promises that his lips will praise the Lord.

3. The POWER Of Praise!

Amazing things happen when I praise the Lord. Psalm 18 says, "I will call upon the Lord who is worthy of praise, and so shall I be saved from my enemies."

Acts 16:25 & 26 tells of Paul and Silas in prison. "At about midnight Paul and Silas were praying and singing hymns to God and the other prisoners were listening to them. Suddenly, there was an earthquake so violent that the foundations of the prison were shaken. At once, all the prison doors flew open and everybody's chains came loose."

Things happen when you praise. God gets involved. Where the Spirit of the Lord is there IS power.

2 Chronicles 20:22 says, "As they began to sing and praise, the Lord set ambushes against the men of Amon...and they were defeated."

After seeing what God can do in my life through praise, I should say as David did in Psalm 71:14, *"I will praise you yet more and more."*

Chapter 29

Special Delivery

Gen. 22:1-14
Now it came about after these things, that God tested Abraham, and said to him, "Abraham!" And he said, "Here I am."

And He said, "Take now your son, your only son, whom you love, Isaac, and go to the land of Moriah; and offer him there as a burnt offering on one of the mountains of which I will tell you."

So Abraham rose early in the morning and saddled his donkey, and took two of his young men with him and Isaac his son; and he split wood for the burnt offering, and arose and went to the place of which God had told him.

...And Abraham took the wood of the burnt offering and laid it on Isaac his son, and he took in his hand the fire and the knife. So the two of them walked on together.

And Isaac spoke to Abraham his father and said, "My father!" And he said, "Here I am, my son." And he said, "Behold, the fire and the wood, but where is the lamb for the burnt offering?"

And Abraham said, "God will provide for Himself the lamb for the burnt offering, my son." So the two of them walked on together.

Then they came to the place of which God had told him; and Abraham built the altar there, and arranged the wood, and bound his son Isaac, and laid him on the altar on top of the wood. And Abraham stretched out his hand, and took the knife to slay his son.

But the angel of the Lord called to him from heaven, and said, "...Do not stretch out your hand against the lad, and do nothing to him; for now I know that you fear God, since you have not withheld your son, your only son, from Me."

Then Abraham raised his eyes and looked, and behold, behind him a ram caught in the thicket by his horns; and Abraham went and took the ram, and offered him up for a burnt offering in the place of his son.

And Abraham called the name of that place The Lord Will Provide, as it is said to this day, "In the mount of the Lord it will be provided." (NAS)

We live in a remarkable society. We have made the delivery of merchandise an art form. Domino's delivers a pizza in 30 minutes or less. Federal Express, UPS and others can deliver a package to the other side of the country over night.

But I've found a delivery service that is better than all of these. Best of all, it's free! It happens in an instant and lasts for an eternity. I'm speaking, of course, of the deliveries from sin provided by the Eternal Creator, Jesus Christ our Lord.

There is a beautiful picture of our deliverance found in Genesis 22. There we find the story of Abraham and Isaac.

We join Abraham after God's promise to him has been fulfilled. Isaac has been born and is growing into a young man when God asks Abraham to sacrifice him on the mountain.

1. Isaac Had An Appointment With Death.
God spoke to Abraham and told him to offer Isaac as a burnt sacrifice. (That is certain death!) Abraham didn't negotiate—he obeyed.

We all have an appointment with death. Hebrews 9:27 says, "It is appointed unto man once to die and then the judgement." Most people act as if they will live forever, but we know there will be an accounting of our lives.

2. Isaac Did Not Know Where Or When.

Isaac was oblivious to the nearness of death. In fact, he helped his dad pack for this trip and thought he was coming along for the ride.

No man knows his appointed time to die. A man's days are numbered by the Lord, and none of us knows his/her allotted time.

3. Isaac Carried His Destruction On His Back.
Genesis 22:6 says that he himself carried the fuel and the knife that would be the death of him.

Each of us carries in his/her mortal body the penalty of death due to sin. It is disobedience to God that testifies against us. "The soul that sinneth, it shall die."

4. *Isaac Was Bound On The Altar.*

Verse 9 says he was bound on the altar and could not save himself. The knife was ready, the fire was prepared and Isaac was helpless.

We all have been bound by our sin and were helpless to save ourselves. Sin's destructive hold cannot be broken on our own.

5. *Isaac Was Delivered From Death By Substitute.*

God provided a substitute to save Isaac's life. God saved him because he was the precious promise and there was a purpose for his life.

We all were spared because of a substitute. 1 Peter 3:18 says, "For Christ died for sins once for all, the righteous for the unrighteous to bring you to God."

You see, we too were a precious promise because we were created for the purpose of fellowship with Him. In other words, He saved us because He loved us.

What a beautiful picture of deliverance. It is indeed a SPECIAL DELIVERY!

Chapter 30

Trying To Do The Job Alone!

Ecclesiastes 4:9-12
Two are better than one because they have a good return for their labor. For if either of them falls, the one will lift up his companion. But woe to the one who falls when there is not another to lift him up.

Furthermore, if two lie down together they keep warm, but how can one be warm alone? And if one can overpower him who is alone, two can resist him. A cord of three strands is not quickly torn apart. (NAS)

"If you want something done right, you just have to do it yourself." Have you ever heard that statement? Have you ever said it or felt it? I think we've all heard, said or felt the frustration of feeling like we have to do something by ourselves.

As a teenager, I was profoundly effected by a story shared with me by my pastor, Milton Krans. I believe you will be challenged by its message as well.

Dear Sir:

I am writing in response to your request for additional information. In block number 3 of the accident report form, I put "trying to do the job alone" as the cause of my accident. You said in your letter that I should explain more fully, and I trust that the following details will be sufficient.

I am a bricklayer by trade. On the date of the accident, I was working alone on the roof of a new 6-story building. When I completed my work, I discovered that I had about 500 pounds of brick left over. Rather than carry the bricks down by hand, I decided to lower them in a barrel by using a pulley which fortunately was attached to the side of the building, at the sixth floor.

Securing the rope at ground level, I went up to the roof, swung the barrel out, and loaded the brick into it. Then I went back to the ground and untied the rope, holding it tightly to insure a slow descent of the 500 pounds of brick. You will note in block number 11 of the accident report form that I weigh 135 pounds.

Due to my surprise at being jerked off the ground so suddenly, I lost my presence of mind and forgot to let go of the rope. Needless to say, I proceeded at a rather rapid rate up the side of the building.

In the vicinity of the third floor, I met the barrel coming down. This explains the fractured skull and broken collarbone. Slowed only slightly, I continued my rapid ascent not stopping until the fingers of my right hand were two knuckles deep into the pulley.

Fortunately, by this time I regained my presence of mind and was able to hold tightly to the rope in spite of my pain.

At approximately the same time, however, the barrel of bricks hit the ground—and the bottom fell out of the barrel. Devoid of the weight of the bricks, the barrel now weighs approximately 50 pounds.

I refer you again to my weight in block number 11. As you might imagine, I began a rapid descent down the side of the building.

In the vicinity of the third floor, I met the barrel coming up. This accounts for the two fractured ankles and the lacerations of my legs and lower body. The encounter with the barrel slowed me enough to lessen my injuries when I fell onto the pile of bricks, and, fortunately, only 3 vertebrae were cracked.

I'm sorry to report, however, that as I lay there on the bricks, in pain, unable to stand, and watching the empty barrel 6 stories above me—I again lost my presence of mind, and...I let go of the rope. The empty barrel weighed more than the rope so it came back down on me and broke both my legs.

I hope I have furnished the information you require as to how the accident occurred.

You might remember this story the next time you are tempted to say, "I'll do it myself." It is important to involve others in our work. Ecclesiastes 4 tells us, "Two are better than one. They receive a good return in their work."

Chapter 31

Thirsty Anyone?

Psalm 42
As the deer pants for the water brooks, so my soul pants for Thee, O God. My soul thirsts for God, for the living God;
When shall I come and appear before God? My tears have been my food day and night, While they say to me all day long, "Where is your God?" These things I remember, and I pour out my soul within me.
For I used to go along with the throng and lead them in procession to the house of God, with the voice of joy and thanksgiving, a multitude keeping festival.
Why are you in despair, O my soul? And why have you become disturbed within me?
Hope in God, for I shall again praise Him for the help of His presence. (NAS).

In this Psalm, we find a statement that has been put to music and sounds very familiar to many, but often passes by our ears and our spirits unnoticed. "As the deer panteth for the water, so my soul longeth after thee...."

It speaks of a deer that is thirsty to the extent of breathing heavily in anticipation of the streams of water. The Psalmist creates a picture for us to see his desire to seek after God.

The next verse lets us see the depth of that desire. "My soul thirsts for God, for the Living God. When can I go and meet God." This "meeting" possibly spoke of his desire to meet God in heaven to spend eternity. Given the Psalmist's statements of his joy in going to the temple, it could refer to his desire to spend time in God's house seeking His face. In either case, his soul's greatest desire—single desire—was to meet with God. The word "pant" means to long, crave, seek out, desire or anticipate. Do any of these words describe your desire for God? Do you long for the next opportunity to go to the house of God to seek Him? When the altar call is made, do you make your way to it as a deer would when it sees a stream?

Are you thirsty for the living water God made available through His only Son? If not, you must create thirst in your life. How can we do this? Well, it is the same way that we develop a craving for anything else. We must taste it the first time, then go back for the second taste, and so on. Once you experience its goodness, pleasure, fulfillment and joy—then you'll want to taste it again and again!

Psalm 34:8 declares this familiar phrase, *"Taste and see that the Lord is good."* Once you have tasted of His goodness, you'll develop a craving for His presence.

CAUTION: Cravings will dissipate if you abstain from partaking of it! Just as cravings for certain foods will vanish after we refuse to eat them for a time, so too will our cravings for God when we absence ourselves from His presence and refrain from tasting of His goodness.

Based upon this caution, we should be careful about absencing ourselves from the presence of the Lord. We should take every opportunity to be in the House of God—the church service—to keep our passion for God fresh.

Chapter 32

Help Wanted–
Inquire Within!

Luke 10:2
And He was saying to them, "The harvest is plentiful, but the laborers are few; therefore beseech the Lord of the harvest to send out laborers into His harvest." (NAS)

I've been around the church most of my life, and it seems we've faced the same challenge from the beginning—we must have help if we're going to complete the job!

I'm reminded of the time when Christ surveyed the ready harvest and the available work force and announced the need for more help. The fields were white and ready, but there were not enough laborers for the job. He symbolically posted a "Help Wanted" ad that appears in every Bible-believing church in the world.

Help Wanted: Advancing kingdom looking for laborers to complete the harvest. Workers must be teachable, dependable, punctual, alert and energetic.
Inquire Within!

This is not an appeal for warm bodies to fill space, but for a viable work force to complete the task of the church.

The church needs workers that are:

Teachable! Workers in God's kingdom must have a willingness to be trained. "Do your best to present yourself to God as one approved. A workman who...correctly handles the word of truth." (2 Tim 2:15)

Loyal! Your allegience must be unquestioned. "No one serving as a soldier gets involved in civilian affairs—he wants to please his commanding officer." (2 Tim 2:24) This is no time for non-committal Christians. Ephesians 6:17 says that we must serve wholeheartedly.

Dependable! Can you be depended upon? As the master entrusted his treasure to his servants in Matthew 25, our Master has entrusted much to us and will demand an accounting of what we've done with it.

Punctual! Our time is nearing an end. "As long as it is day, we must do the work of him who sent me. Night is coming when no one can work." (Jn. 9:4)

Alert! We do not know when the master will return, or what attack the enemy will launch against us. We must be alert and ready for action. (Mt. 13:33; Eph. 6:18; 1 Thess. 5:6)

Energetic! We must be excited about our product if we ever expect anyone else to be. I know of no other way to be dynamic and spirited than to be filled with the Holy Spirit. Acts 1:8 says that we would receive power when the Holy Spirit came upon us to be witnesses of Christ. We see the believers of the early church moving in boldness and power to reach the lost.

If the church could develop a work force with these qualities, there would be no limits to all we can accomplish for the Kingdom of God!

Chapter 33

Someone's In The Kitchen With Martha!

Luke 10:38-42
Now as they were traveling along, He entered a certain village; and a woman named Martha welcomed Him into her home. And she had a sister called Mary, who moreover was listening to the Lord's word, seated at His feet.

But Martha was distracted with all her preparations; and she came up to Him, and said, "Lord, do You not care that my sister has left me to do all the serving alone? Then tell her to help me."

But the Lord answered and said to her, "Martha, Martha, you are worried and bothered about so many things; but only a few things are necessary, really only one, for Mary has chosen the good part, which shall not be taken away from her." (NAS)

I've often imagined what it must have been like to live in the day of Jesus and to have experienced His ministry first hand—WOW! I have even used the illustration, "What if Jesus came to your house? What would you do? How would you behave?"

Well, in Luke 10 it happened in the lives of Mary and Martha. Their brother Lazarus was a close friend of Jesus and one day He came home with him. Imagine the two scenes:

(scene 1—the kitchen)

Martha is there, building a fire, peeling potatoes, cutting the vegetables with stacks of pots and pans. The more she worked, the more tired she became. The more tired she became, the more frustrated she became.

(scene 2—the living room)

Jesus and his followers are there on the couch and the floor, magazines and papers cluttered on the coffee table and Mary is sitting in the floor in front of Jesus just listening.

Martha finally snapped! "Jesus, tell her to come and help me!" What did Jesus say to her? (v. 41-42) Martha, Martha! You are troubled by many things, but one thing is needed...Mary has chosen that thing. He was literally telling her, "You are worried, focused and distracted by many things, but only one thing is necessary (important or has priority)! Mary has chosen that thing!"

You see, God isn't telling us that works aren't important, but He is telling us that the more important thing is time in His presence. It's not the stuff you do that is important to God—it is YOU!

The problem is, there are those who prefer to work an 8 hour shift of hard labor for God than spend time in His presence. These are the same people who can walk the mall for two hours, mow the lawn, stand in the kitchen and clean the house, but are too tired to stand 10, 15 or 20 minutes worshipping God in church.

Why? Because most people are intimidated by intimacy with God. He often reveals things that are unpleasant or uncomfortable. Often, He asks us to do difficult things that demand that we trust in Him.

Someone's in the kitchen with Martha! Her story describes your life—serving, doing, lifting and carrying—only to be left drained, frustrated and maybe a little bitter. You've probably read the story and said to yourself, *"Yeah! Why doesn't Mary help her sister!"*

God is speaking to your heart to Come Out Of The Kitchen!

Someone's In The Kitchen With Martha, **But WHO's IN The LIVINGROOM With Mary?** The living room symbolizes the priority of time in His presence, listening to His voice and learning His ways.

How about coming out of the kitchen and into the livingroom for a time of refreshing. You will then have the strength and effectiveness to return to your work!

Chapter 34

Why Sit We Here 'Til They Die?

2 Kings 7:3-9
Now there were four leprous men at the entrance of the gate; and they said to one another, "Why do we sit here until we die? If we say, `We will enter the city,' then the famine is in the city and we shall die there; and if we sit here, we die also. Now therefore come, and let us go over to the camp of the Arameans. If they spare us, we shall live; and if they kill us, we shall but die."

And they arose at twilight to go to the camp of the Arameans; when they came to the outskirts of the camp of the Arameans, behold, there was no one there. For the Lord had caused the army of the Arameans to hear a sound of chariots and a sound of horses, even the sound of a great army, so that they said to one another, "Behold, the king of Israel has hired against us the kings of the Hittites and the kings of the Egyptians, to come upon us." Therefore they arose and fled in the twilight, and left their tents and their horses and their donkeys, even the camp just as it was, and fled for their life.

When these lepers came to the outskirts of the camp, they entered one tent and ate and drank, and carried from there silver and gold and clothes, and went and hid them; and they returned and entered another tent and carried from there also, and went and hid them.

Then they said to one another, "We are not doing right. This day is a day of good news, but we are keeping silent; if we wait until morning light, punishment will overtake us. Now therefore come, let us go and tell the king's household."

It doesn't take a rocket scientist to realize that we live in a world of hurting people who need help, hope and healing. Realizing that fact and doing something about it are very different, however.

It seems that if we believe that the Bible is really true, then we will also believe that all have sinned—sin demands death—and God's gift is eternal life—and whosoever believeth in him shall not perish but have everlasting life. If so, WHY SIT WE HERE 'TIL THEY DIE?

2 Kings 7 tells the story of four lepers who were living outside the camp of Israel during a time of famine. Their enemies had put them under siege and were starving them to defeat. Their plan was nearly working when we meet the four lepers.

Being lepers, they were outcasts of society and were forced to live outside the city. They depended upon food from the city and it was no longer available. At the point of starvation, they were meeting about what they should do. Finally, one of the men said, "Hey! We can't go on like this. If we stay here, we'll die. If we go to the city, we'll die there. Why not just go to our enemies' camp. The worst they could do is kill us. Why sit we here until we die?"

As the story goes, they walked to the camp of their enemies and as they walked, the Lord caused them to hear the sound of chariots and soldiers marching. Thinking that the neighboring enemies were coming in upon them they fled their camp killing each other in the confusion. By the time the four lepers arrived, the camp was desserted and all that remained was the food and treasure! This is amazing in itself, but the point of the story is yet to come.

As they were stuffing themselves with food and dragging off the treasure one of them said, "We are not doing right! We must tell our fellow countrymen about this or we will be responsible for their destruction."

You see, this is a picture of the world and the church. The world is in the midst of famine where they hunger for satisfaction and fulfillment but never find it. Their hunger has caused them to stoop to such disgusting levels of sin to quench the emptiness, but they never find help.

The church represents the four lepers who have found the answer and are feasting on the bounty of God's provision but the world still hungers near death.

We must tell them where they can find food to quench their emptiness. How can we do that? What must we do?

1. ***We Must LIVE It!*** We must show the light of God's love in our lives so they can see His love for them (Mt. 5:15-16) They are looking for Christians who really live what they say they believe.
2. ***We Must LOVE Them!*** 1 Corinthians 13 tells us that without love, nothing we do matters. We can speak in tongues, explain mysteries, move mountains and give all we possess to the poor, but without love, it is all empty and hollow.
3. ***We Must LOOK To Others' Needs!*** Philippians 2:4 tells us to "not only look to our own interests, but to the needs and interests of others." And Gal. 6:10 says, "as we have opportunity, let us do good to all."
4. ***We Must LEAD Them!*** Jesus said in Acts 1:8 that we were to "be witnesses unto Me." We must lead people to Him. We cannot lead them to us—we can't meet their needs. We cannot lead them to doctrine—doctrine doesn't save. We cannot lead them to the church—the church cannot bring life to them. We MUST lead them to CHRIST!

Why sit we here 'til they die? We have a responsibility to tell the good news of eternal life to the starving world around us!

Chapter 35

Eyeball To Knee Cap

1 Sam 17:47-47
Then the Philistine came on and approached David, with the shield-bearer in front of him. When the Philistine looked and saw David, he disdained him; for he was but a youth, and ruddy, with a handsome appearance.

And the Philistine said to David, "Am I a dog, that you come to me with sticks?" And the Philistine cursed David by his gods. The Philistine also said to David, "Come to me, and I will give your flesh to the birds of the sky and the beasts of the field."

Then David said to the Philistine, "You come to me with a sword, a spear, and a javelin, but I come to you in the name of the Lord of hosts, the God of the armies of Israel, whom you have taunted. This day the Lord will deliver you up into my hands, and I will strike you down and remove your head from you. And I will give the dead bodies of the army of the Philistines this day to the birds of the sky and the wild beasts of the earth, that all the earth may know that there is a God in Israel, and that all this assembly may know that the Lord does not deliver by sword or by spear; for the battle is the Lord's and He will give you into our hands." (NAS)

Have you ever faced something that was bigger than yourself? Life is full of experiences like that. At times, problems, turmoil and sickness seem to tower over us like a giant. The challenges appear to be insurmountable.

That must have been what the showdown between David and Goliath must have looked like. David met his giant in the valley of Elah and stared at him EYEBALL TO KNEE CAP.

You see, Goliath was 9 feet tall. That's almost the size of an NBA basketball goal. We're not sure how tall David was, but he was probably not much more than half that tall. In spite of this, he met the giant with boldness and confidence because he knew what most people had forgotten—the battle wasn't his, it was the Lord's!

David didn't pick the fight. This Philistine had defied the God of the Israelites and God was going to settle this. David didn't need technological weapons or fancy armor. He marched into battle with nothing but the name of the Lord and a few smooth rocks.

Face it, all of us have battles. You can be on the top of the mountain and...boom! The "giant" will show up to bring you down. The enemy of our souls, Satan, will pick a fight with us because he wants to keep us from experiencing God's best in our lives. Ephesians 6:10-11 reminds us that we are in a constant battle for our souls and the enemy will use any means to defeat us. He will use finances, job difficulties, family crises or anything else. They will be "giant" problems, but we must face them EYEBALL TO KNEE CAP!

You'll be tempted to give up. However, you must have confidence that the battle is not yours—it is GOD'S!

It doesn't matter how large your giant may be. It doesn't matter how strong your enemy may appear. God is in charge! David writes in Psalm 18 that, *"The Lord is my rock, my fortress and my deliverer...I will call upon the Lord...so shall I be saved from my enemies."* David knew that God would always be with him in the midst of battle and deliver him.

Jeremiah knew the same thing. The Lord spoke in Jeremiah 1:8, "Do not be afraid of their faces, for I am with you to deliver you."

Be confident in the fact that your battle may be too big for you—but it is never too big for the strength and might of our God. We are victorious in Him!

David faced his giant "EYEBALL TO KNEE CAP" that day. Onlookers were prepared for the little guy to be torn to pieces, but it was Goliath who lost his head!

We would do well to remember that the next time we face our giants.

Chapter 36

We Need Eleven Heads Of Let-Us!

Often when we are looking for ways to remember things, it is helpful to use a word picture or word game to assist us. That's what this month's title does for us—it helps us remember ELEVEN challenges from Hebrews that begin with "Let Us." If we can make them a part of our lives, they will help mature us in our spiritual walk.

The Author uses the phrase "Let Us" to pull us together as Christians and to prod us to a consistent testimony for Christ. Regardless of what anyone else is doing:

1. *Let Us...Be Careful!* (Hebrews 4:1)

Be careful to not fall short of the "rest" that Christ has for us—Heaven!

2. *Let Us...Work*! (Hebrews 4:11)

Let us make every effort—or do what we must do to make it to heaven. The author of Hebrews also uses the word "diligence" in living our Christian lives.

3. *Let Us...Approach the throne of Grace!* (Hebrews 4:16)

Don't just talk about our needs—pray about them. Christians often want to talk about something more than doing the one thing that brings change—pray!

4. *Let Us...Go On To Maturity*! (Hebrews 6:1)

It's time for us to move into some deeper spiritual things instead of learning the same "elementary" things about God.

5. *Let Us...Draw Near To God!* (Hebrews 10:22)

With a sincere heart and full assurance we must draw close to God. It's time to distance ourselves from the world and live fully for God. James 4:8 says, if we draw closer to him, God will draw closer to us.

6. Let Us...Hold Unswervingly To Our Faith! (Hebrews 10:23)

The one who promised is faithful. His promises are not flimsy or hollow. Don't let them go.

7. Let Us...Consider One Another! (Hebrews 10:24-25)

We must look to the needs of others! We must spur them on to love and good deeds. As a bonus it says, "let us not give up meeting together, but rather let us encourage one another." Our church attendance is important to people who count on us and are encouraged when they see us.

8. Let Us...Throw Off Every Hinderance! (Hebrews 12:1)

We must get rid of the sins and entanglements that keep us from living for God. They could be hobbies or relationships that compete for our time with God.

9. Let Us...Worship! (Hebrews 12:28)

Come to Him in reverence and awe, because He is a consuming fire!

10. Let Us...Go Forth! (13:13)

We must press toward Him and push beyond our comfort zones. We must be willing to be laughed at if necessary.

11. Let us...Offer A Sacrifice Of Praise! (Hebrews 13:15)

Praise to God should be a fruit of our lips, which means: Praise should continually flow from our mouths as a natural process of serving him. What's on the inside WILL spill out. If we are full of Him, then His goodness comes out of us.

These are some great encouragements for the church today! We need Eleven Heads of "LET US" to make a complete salad—or to be a complete church before the Master!

Chapter 37

Isaiah's Corrected Vision

Isaiah 6:1-8

In the year of King Uzziah's death, I saw the Lord sitting on a throne, lofty and exalted, with the train of His robe filling the temple.

Seraphim stood above Him, each having six wings; with two he covered his face, and with two he covered his feet, and with two he flew.

And one called out to another and said, "Holy, Holy, Holy, is the Lord of hosts, the whole earth is full of His glory."

And the foundations of the thresholds trembled at the voice of him who called out, while the temple was filling with smoke.

Then I said, "Woe is me, for I am ruined! Because I am a man of unclean lips, and I live among a people of unclean lips; For my eyes have seen the King, the Lord of hosts."

Then one of the seraphim flew to me, with a burning coal in his hand which he had taken from the altar with tongs. And he touched my mouth with it and said, "Behold, this has touched your lips; and your iniquity is taken away, and your sin is forgiven."

Then I heard the voice of the Lord, saying, "Whom shall I send, and who will go for Us?" Then I said, "Here am I. Send me!" (NAS)

We've all heard the stories of children who began struggling in school only to find that their problems were vision related. They began to fall behind because they couldn't see the assignments on the chalkboard. Once they had their vision corrected with glasses, they improved.

Scripture tells the story of a young prophet who was in danger of falling behind, and as it turns out, he needed his vision corrected too.

Records indicate that Isaiah lived during the last twenty years of the reign of King Uzziah. His reign began well and he accomplished a great deal, but 2 Chronicles 26:16 says "But after Uzziah became powerful his pride led to his downfall." Isaiah saw his decline. While he still looked successful, he was not what he once was. He had done so much for Judah only to be struck with leprosy in his last few years of reign because of unfaithfulness. Isaiah was disillusioned to see this once great king living in a separate house, unable to enter his own palace.

Isaiah needed to see something before he began to fall behind spiritually. He needed a correction in his vision. Isaiah 6 gives us the details on the awakening that changed his life, and the future of Israel.

Isaiah Had His Focus Adjusted!

In verse 1 Isaiah declares, "I saw the Lord!" Until this moment, Isaiah didn't have his focus upon the Lord, but upon king Uzziah. It wasn't until he was out of the way that Isaiah was able to see the Holy One high and lifted up. The angels cried "Holy," and it shook the door-posts and filled the room with smoke.

Until you and I see the Lord for who He really is, we are destined for disillusionment.

He Came To Terms With His Flaws!

In Isaiah 6:5 he declares, "Woe is me—I am ruined! For I am a man of unclean lips and I dwell among a people of unclean lips." He realized that he was sinful. He realized that he was not perfect and that he was miserably short of where God wanted him to be.

When we're faced with a Holy God, we realize our righteousness is as filthy rags. We must come to terms with our own flaws and quit justifying them. 1 John 1:8 says, "If we claim to be without sin, we deceive ourselves and the truth is not in us.

He Surrendered His Future!

Isaiah said in verse 8, "...I heard the voice of the Lord saying 'Whom shall I send? And who will go for us?' and I said Here I am, send me."

God calls out, "whom shall I send?" The gospel must go forth. The message must be told. Who will accept the challenge and go?

Isaiah accepted the challenge and surrendered his future. How about us?

We must have an awakening that will correct our vision as a church. It requires us to <u>Adjust</u> our **Focus**...<u>Come to terms</u> with our **Flaws**...and <u>Surrender</u> our **Future!**

Chapter 38

Making Room For God

2 Kings 4:8-10
Now there came a day when Elisha passed over to Shunem, where there was a prominent woman, and she persuaded him to eat food. And so it was, as often as he passed by, he turned in there to eat food.

And she said to her husband, "Behold now, I perceive that this is a holy man of God passing by us continually.

"Please, let us make a little walled upper chamber and let us set a bed for him there, and a table and a chair and a lampstand; and it shall be, when he comes to us, that he can turn in there." (NAS)

It is amazing to see the number of home improvement shows on television today. I enjoy watching and dreaming that I could do some of the projects they demonstrate. I am certain my skills are not advanced to the level of Bob Villa, Dean Johnson, or even Tim "the tool man" Taylor for that matter—but a guy can dream, huh? The projects I am most amazed with are the ones that involve an addition to an existing home.

You probably didn't realize it, but television didn't start the "home improvement" concept. In 2 Kings 4, we find a family that made the decision to add a room to their home for a very worthy purpose. There we find a woman and her family adding a room for the prophet Elisha.

This may not seem like a big deal, but when you realize the sacrifice of adding a room on to their house, this begins to take on a greater significance. Since the prophet was the man of God, this Shunammite woman was literally making (a) room for the presence of God in their lives. By this act, making room for God, she opened the door to the blessings upon her home.

After the addition was complete, Elisha came for a visit and entered the room for the first time. He immediately called for the Shunammite woman and said, "You have gone to all this trouble for us. Now what can be done for you?" After inquiring of her, Elisha's servant reported that she had no child and that her husband was old. He called for her and prophesied, "About this time next year...you will hold a son in your arms." Sure enough, by that time the next year, she had a son.

There is so much more to the story than we have time to share, but I am greatly impressed by the fact that this act of sacrifice—making room for the presence of God—brought blessing to their lives. This should cause us to consider what we could do to bring blessing upon our lives.

The key is in the title—*Making Room For God!* As men and women desiring to please God, we must look for ways to "make room" in our lives for God. This might not require building a room onto the house for the prophet, but it could require us to *move some stuff out* of our lives that crowd out the presence of the Lord.

Isaiah 57:15 says, "I dwell in the high and holy place...with him also that is of a contrite and humble spirit...to revive the spirit of the humble and revive the heart of the contrite." The simple fact is that God desires to dwell with and in us—not in temples built with hands. This literally means that God desires to dwell with those who have made room for Him and desire Him to be there.

"Making room" speaks of accommodation, which means "to make provision for." In light of the move of God's Spirit around us and allowing His presence into our daily lives, we must all make the adjustments necessary to let God move in us.

What will you have to do to make room for God's presence in your life? It might require something as simple as rearranging some things, but it might also require some major construction. Either way, I'm confident that God will bless those who make room for him!

Chapter 39

David's Giants

1 Samuel 17:32-33
And David said to Saul, "Let no man's heart fail on account of him; your servant will go and fight with this Philistine."

Then Saul said to David, "You are not able to go against this Philistine to fight with him; for you are but a youth while he has been a warrior from his youth." (NAS)

Since my earliest remembrances of being in church I have enjoyed hearing the story of David and Goliath. His cool attitude and strength in the face of danger is an inspiration to all of us when we encounter "giant problems" of our own.

The Scripture says that David said to Saul, "Let no one lose heart on account of this Philistine. Your servant will go and fight him." What gave him the confidence? How did he develop the determination to make such a statement?

Was it the lion and bear he had killed years earlier?

Was it the anointing that he had received from the prophet Samuel?

Or was it the prize of winning Saul's daughter to the prevailing warrior?

I'm sure that these could have been helpful, but I don't believe any of these was the key ingredient. I believe it was his giant killing experience. You might ask, "What giant killing experience? The Bible doesn't mention any other giant than Goliath!" Oh, but it does.

You see, if David didn't overcome the other giants in his life, he wouldn't have been able to face Goliath. So, what were the other giants? I must admit they weren't physical ones, but they were giant issues in David's life. They're the same ones we each face in our own lives.

His First Giant—Submission To Authority! (1 Sam. 17:17-19) David played by the rules. Even after receiving the anointing upon his life, he tended his father's sheep. He submitted to Saul's authority even though he was trying to kill him.

There are a number of people who miss their appointment with greatness because they cannot follow authority. David killed that giant by learning submission early in life!

His Second Giant—Self Discipline! (1 Sam. 17:20) He got up early and obeyed his father. This showed his diligence. He cared for the sheep of his father. This showed his responsibility.

Self discipline is the key to achieving any success in life. Without discipline we would all be out of control.

His Third Giant—Soldiers Who Were Indifferent! (1 Sam 17: 24) David arrived at the scene of the battle to find that everyone was terrified and refused to fight. It would have been easy for him to join in with the crowd and say, "If no one else is going to do anything, then why should I?" But David said, "Is there not a cause?" He was not going to let "everyone else" determine his destiny.

Sometimes we must rise above the apathy around us to accomplish victory.

His Fourth Giant—Someone's Rejection! (1 Sam 17:28-29) Little brothers often look up to their older brothers, and I'm sure that David did too. When his brother asked him, "Why are you here?" it was insulting to David. Then his brother told him to go back and tend his "few" sheep. David's response was, "Now what have I done?"

He was rejected by someone he cared about, but he went out and faced the battle anyway.

His Fifth Giant—Substitution Or Something For God's Power! (1 Sam 17:38-39) Saul offered David the use of his armor in battle. Saul was probably trying to minimize the liability if David should be killed, but it wasn't David's size.

I'm sure it was tempting to hide in something for protection, but David was going into battle in the name of the Lord. He knew that God's protection was sufficient.

So many times, we try to enter battle in our own strength or in someone else's strength. God is sufficient!

In the final analysis, we must defeat these giants in our lives to be victorious in our toughest battles. If we can defeat them, we'll have the determination to face Goliath in God's power and strength.

Chapter 40

Church On The Move?
OR
Church On The Stay?

Acts 2:42-47
And they were continually devoting themselves to the apostles' teaching and to fellowship, to the breaking of bread and to prayer.

And everyone kept feeling a sense of awe; and many wonders and signs were taking place through the apostles.

And all those who had believed were together, and had all things in common; and they began selling their property and possessions, and were sharing them with all, as anyone might have need.

And day by day continuing with one mind in the temple, and breaking bread from house to house, they were taking their meals together with gladness and sincerity of heart, praising God, and having favor with all the people. And the Lord was adding to their number day by day those who were being saved. (NAS)

Rev. 3:15-17
I know your deeds, that you are neither cold nor hot; I would that you were cold or hot. So because you are lukewarm, and neither hot nor cold, I will spit you out of My mouth. Because you say, "I am rich, and have become wealthy, and have need of nothing," and you do not know that you are wretched and miserable and poor and blind and naked. (NAS)

We have all seen the type of churches mentioned in our title above. We have seen churches that are growing and have vital ministry to their communities, but we have also seen churches that are happy and content to stay the same from year to year. We find in our text, that the Word of God addresses these two types of churches. If we will look closely, we will find some very startling patterns to watch for in our own churches.

Revelation 3 tells of the church at Laodocia. It is a church that has become satisfied with staying the same. It is a very common church in today's society where we judge success in having the same attendance as we did last year. The Laodocian church settled for "warm" rather than "hot!"

Contrastly, Acts 2 tells of a very young church that is adding daily to their numbers. It is a vibrant, growing, and moving church that is consumed with reaching the world. If I were to ask parishioners or pastors of most churches which type of church they would like to have, I think they would respond that they want the Acts 2 type church, but aren't sure how to get there.

Acts 2:42 says, *"They devoted themselves to the apostles teaching and to the fellowship, to the breaking of bread and to prayer."* These are key ingredients. Sound teaching, fellowship and prayer. But what else is there? Verses 43-46 give us the remaining ingredients.

Verse 43—EVERYONE was filled with awe...
Verse 44—All the believers had EVERYTHING in common...
Verse 45—They gave to ANYONE as he had need...
Verse 46—EVERY DAY they continued to meet together...

EVERYONE—means the church was undivided. We were told in Acts 2:1 that they were in one place and in one accord. If churches are going to move forward, the people must be in unity. It doesn't mean that they will agree on everything, but they will be going in the same direction together.

EVERYTHING—means they were unrestrained. Basically, what they had was not nearly as important as what they were striving to achieve. They were committed to sacrifice whatever it took to reach those in need. The church of Jesus Christ must be willing to sacrifice everything to take the gospel to our world. If we are not willing, then our things mean more to us than souls.

ANYONE—means they were unrestrictive. The word "whosoever" applied to anyone needing to hear the gospel. It wasn't dependent upon their social or economic status. Sadly, the church has a reputation for "playing favorites."

Too often, we have selectively shared the gospel with those we felt were deserving.

EVERY DAY—means they were <u>unfailing.</u> This speaks of consistency. Their testimony was consistent from day to day. Psalm 1 talks of one whose leaf does not wither. Regardless of the heat or challenge around us—the church must remain consistent! We serve a Savior who is the same yesterday, today, and forever—why should we be different from one day to the next?

If each church could incorporate these four words into its way of living, along with sound teaching, fellowship and prayer—the gospel will be advanced. We will not be a church on the stay, but on the move!

Additional copies of this book
may be obtained by
contacting the author:

Gregory S. Perkins